Advance Praise for

Living Large

"Ray Albrektson has been a dear friend and fellow servant of the Lord for many years. By personal experience and knowledge, he is eminently qualified to write this book, offering golden nuggets of wisdom about how to be full of joy and effective with whatever God provides. Highly recommended."

> —BILL BRIGHT
> founder and president, Campus Crusade for Christ International

"*Living Large* is filled with pure biblical common sense that will help readers discover the simple secrets of financial happiness."

> —JOSH MCDOWELL
> president, Josh McDowell Ministry

"Ray Albrektson is on target! In his thorough and informative style, Ray helps young couples start their marriages off on the right foot by giving them a clear plan for their finances. This book should be given to every couple, *before* they get married!"

> —DENNIS RAINEY
> author, speaker, host of the *Family Life Today* radio program, and head of Family Life Conferences

"You will appreciate Ray's humor, powerful message, real-life stories, and practical principles—but most of all his heart for God."

> —ETHAN POPE
> author of *How to Be a Smart Money Manager* and president, Foundations for Living

"Ray Albrektson's suggestions are so valuable because they come from his life experiences and they are biblically based. Financial management is such a major issue in our personal lives that I plan to buy a copy of Ray's book for each of the college students who attend a Bible study I lead."

> —TED BENNA
> president, 401(k) Association, creator of the first 401(k) savings plan

"*Living Large* provides immensely practical and well-proven counsel—from getting out of credit card debt to investing wisely, from giving cheerfully and expectantly to choosing between renting or buying a home. This book tells us how to do it!

"Are you ready to choose your own lifestyle of giving, saving, and spending that is in line with biblical principles? Are you in need of some tried and true steps to do this? Then this book is your starting point for 'living large'!"

—GREGG R. ALLISON, PH.D.
associate professor of theology and church history,
Western Seminary

"The combination of *Living Large*'s spiritual and intensely practical focus gives the proper light to the various components of finances, not an easy task in today's world. I particularly appreciated the joy of living that comes through in Ray's writing. But the best thing I can say about Ray's book is that our son, in his twenties and just starting out, asked to keep the manuscript and is in the process of setting up several of Ray's suggestions. In his words: 'Ray's prescriptions are both radical and freeing.'"

—DR. RON JENSON
author of *Make a Life, Not Just a Living* and chairman,
Future Achievement International, High/Ground Associates

Living Large

How to Live Well—
Even on a Little

Living
Large

J. Raymond
Albrektson

WATERBROOK
PRESS

LIVING LARGE
PUBLISHED BY WATERBROOK PRESS
5446 North Academy Boulevard, Suite 200
Colorado Springs, Colorado 80918
A division of Random House, Inc.

Scripture taken from the *Holy Bible, New International Version*®. NIV®
Copyright © 1973, 1978, 1984 by International Bible Society. Used by
permission of Zondervan Publishing House. All rights reserved.

ISBN 1-57856-227-9

Library of Congress Cataloging-in-Publication Data
Albrektson, Ray.
    Living large : how to live well—even on a little / Ray Albrektson.—1st ed.
        p.   cm.
    ISBN 1-57856-227-9 (pbk.)
    1. Finance, Personal—Religious aspects—Christianity. 2. Consumption (Economics)—
Religious aspects—Christianity. I. Title. II. Title: How to live well—even on a little.
HG179.A424   1999
332.024—dc21   99-44168
                                                                          CIP

Printed in the United States of America
2000—First Edition

10 9 8 7 6 5 4 3 2 1

To my wife, Kathy,

whose character, love, and walk with God
have always been my greatest treasures

Contents

Acknowledgments

I want to thank that wonderfully creative group, Plot & Blot Society, especially my mentors and models, Gary Stanley, Alan Scholes, and Janet Kobobel Grant.

I'm grateful to my children, Laurie and Josh, for allowing Kathy and me to experiment on them while we practiced the principles in this book.

I'm greatly indebted to my editors at WaterBrook Press, especially the cheerfully talented Traci Mullins, for sifting the wheat from vast quantities of chaff.

Finally, countless thanks to my extended family and others who read *Living Large* when it was only a collection of personal letters. Without their encouragement, suggestions, and demand for publication, this book would never have emerged from the circle of my immediate family.

Introduction

Living Large and Loving It

Before my twenty-two-year-old nephew got married last year, his father told him, "Before you say your vows, you need to talk to Ray and Kathy about how to manage your finances!" While I was honored that my brother-in-law considered my wife and me to be wise financial stewards, I felt a bit uncomfortable being held up as a role model. Could I really communicate sound principles of financial management to others, especially the younger generation, in a way that was biblical, practical, and effective? Was I qualified for such a task? After all, I'm not a financial whiz; I don't have a business degree; I'm not rich. My professional expertise has been focused on people, not dollars.

However, as I reflected on the twenty-nine years my wife and I have spent managing our own resources, I realized that we might indeed have some sound advice to offer others who want to avoid common financial difficulties and live happily and successfully on what they earn. Kathy and I couldn't help but notice through the years that most of our friends and college classmates earned far more than we did, yet their financial affairs were usually in a state of chaos. For the past twenty-four years, Kathy and I have earned a very modest missionary salary, yet despite our limited income, we have been able to give generously, save for our children's education and our retirement, and live joyfully on the rest. I realized that perhaps my greatest credential for teaching others what I have learned is having successfully lived by the principles I espouse.

Those who have been quietly successful at managing their finances seldom go around trumpeting the secrets of their success. But maybe they should! I would have loved to have learned from them myself—and not just from those who have been successful in managing large amounts of money, but from those who have seen some success with small incomes. Almost all of us start our earning careers with small incomes, and we financial small fry have the greatest need for motivation and education regarding money management.

Most books on finances tell readers how to make more or spend less. *Living Large: How to Live Well—Even on a Little* concentrates on how to enjoy life to the fullest with whatever God has provided. Jammed with simple and practical ways to organize one's financial life around biblical principles, *Living Large* focuses on how to be a wise steward as well as how to find contentment at any standard of living, at any stage of life.

If you're just beginning your adult life, you will find in these pages the practical orientation you need to make wise financial decisions early, thereby sidestepping potential economic disasters in later years. If you're like many of the young couples and singles I know, you don't want to repeat the mistakes you've seen many older people make with their resources. You're searching for practical, realistic, and down-to-earth guidance on how to put your financial house in order.

If you've already been earning a living for a number of years, you will also find lots of helpful guidance ahead. You'll discover that it's never too late to begin living joyfully on what you have while still giving generously and saving wisely for the future.

I know from experience that it is possible to learn practical strategies for "living large" whether your income is large or small. If you want to have a better understanding of the Bible's teaching on wealth, giving, saving, and spending, then sit down with me for what I hope will be an invaluable introduction to the basic principles of personal finance that Kathy and I have used successfully for over a quarter of a century. If "poor missionaries" can live large by following the principles in this book, then anyone can!

SECTION 1

———

WEALTH 101

Chapter 1

"Don't Touch That— It's Mine!"

I confess—I've always loved junk food. For much of my childhood I spent summers with my grandmother, who lived on a small lake in Michigan. Since I had no allowance, I would periodically scour the neighborhood for empty soft-drink bottles to redeem for candy at the little store at the lake. I recall how hard it was to choose from the vast array of grape balls, wax bottles filled with mysterious syrupy liquids, powdered candies, licorice whips, red vines, and countless other varieties of junk food. It never for a second occurred to me that perhaps I shouldn't even buy the candy!

Our modern world is very similar to that old-fashioned candy counter. Madison Avenue confronts us daily with a great number of purchasing choices. We are constantly barraged with messages telling us, "You should buy this shampoo…this car…this house." The options are staggering. We are *never* told, "Perhaps you should buy nothing, and be content with what you have."

My point is not that we should never spend money or enjoy what we have. But I do believe that there is a more fundamental question at stake than, "Which item should I buy?" As people entrusted with resources that ultimately belong to our Creator, the question we should ask instead is, "Should I buy at all?"

Yesterday I browsed the magazines for sale in my local supermarket. Some touted health and fitness, but as I perused the photos of the muscled individuals inside, I felt increasingly dissatisfied with my present, very adequate body. As I went on to tour the automobile, skiing, photography, and flying magazines, I was inundated with a series of pitches to upgrade my car, get new skis and a head-mounted video camera, and fly my new airplane to Vail to try out all my new goodies! I could not find a single magazine that promoted contentment or living wisely on a modest income.

Well, that kind of magazine would never sell, you might be thinking. And why should it? After all, we don't live in a society that applauds or rewards "modest" earning power. Nor are we encouraged to save or give before we've met all our current "needs"—a term with many definitions, by the way. It's natural to feel pressure to do whatever we can to make sure we're among the "haves" rather than the "have-nots." And isn't that a worthy goal?

I believe the answer to that question depends on our answer to a much bigger one: How does our identity in Christ influence the way we view worldly wealth (or the lack of it)?

When our children, Josh and Laurie, were little, they each had special possessions. Josh loved his Legos, and Laurie had a "Teddy Chair" in which she would sit entranced, watching *Mister Rogers.* As soon as they grew old enough to understand the meaning of the word *mine*, I found I could easily tease them by touching one of their special possessions and asking, "Mine?" They would immediately fire back, "Mine!" and remove my hand.

Like them, I think most of us master the concept of ownership pretty early in life, but as adults, we seldom completely grasp the implications of God's ownership of us. I want to get a bit more theological here and explore two biblical principles of ownership that, if ignored, will sabotage our attempts to live joyfully and contentedly on God's provision.

The first principle—often mentioned in "stewardship" messages—is that *all wealth belongs to God*. Let's face it—there isn't anything of value that God didn't create. Consider the material things of value: tracts of timber, minerals, water, energy sources (solar, fossil fuels), and plants and animals for food. They are all his creation.

For those who would say, "Well, I admit those things may originate with God, but what I earn with the sweat of my brow and my own two hands and on my own time is mine!" I would ask, "Who made your hands? Who gave you your talent?" And as for working on one's "own time," isn't time itself the creation of God? It is being extended second by second purely by his grace, and when he so chooses, it will come to a screeching halt—for each of us.

Soon after God created Adam and Eve, he gave them a simple job description: to care for the garden he had created. Ownership wasn't an issue; I doubt that it would have entered the original couple's heads to imagine that they "owned" any portion of creation. They were managers or stewards, not owners. In fact, the word "stewardship" simply means "to care for another's wealth."

Somehow, probably as a result of the Fall, the concept of ownership became a fact of human experience. And as with so many aspects of fallen humanity, God has chosen to work within the human framework that recognizes the validity of the ownership of things. When we become Christians, however, we experience fundamental changes in the way we possess those things.

This brings us to the second principle of ownership, which is that *we belong to God.* When we experience spiritual birth through faith in Christ, several key transformations take place within us, including our death, burial, and resurrection with Christ. We have become "new creations" as a result of being in Christ; "the old has gone, the new has come" (2 Corinthians 5:17). Prior to our regeneration we were slaves to sin—sin owned us and could control us as it wished. Through death we have been freed from slavery to sin, but through death we have also given up personal ownership of all that was "ours" before.

These theological truths are crucial to good financial management, but they are even more important as a foundation for living joyfully as a Christian. It is only because of who we are in Christ that we have all the important riches God wants us to have: forgiveness of sin, a new life of freedom and grace, and a new relationship to the rest of God's creation.

When we are made new creations in Christ, the first valuable thing God entrusts us with is our own bodies, and the second valuable thing is whatever time he allots that body before it dies. That's why Paul in Romans 12:1-2 exhorted his readers to regard themselves as living sacrifices or, in more modern terms, as "dead men walking." The sacrificed individual now belongs to God, not his former owner. If the Lord doesn't immediately take that sacrifice to himself in heaven, then the person is obligated to continue to live, but to live for the sake of his new owner.

This is the critical center of any Christian theology of wealth, because it makes it clear that the first thing that must be given to God is one's own self and one's own time. As Christians we have no assets of our "own" because through our union with Christ in his death, we died and forfeited the right to our possessions. Through our union with Christ in his resurrection, we became slaves of Christ, empowered by the Holy Spirit to live righteous lives. All that we receive in life is a gift from God, and our measure of wealth is no exception. Just because we still have access to the wealth we formerly "owned" does not mean that it is our possession; it belongs to God just as we belong to him. While the non-Christian talks about earning his daily bread, the Christian knows that the Lord gives us our daily bread. This fundamental fact—that *as Christians we own nothing*—is the theological basis for the principles of wealth management I'll be discussing in this book.

If we are God's property, then all that we earn with our bodies, minds, and time is also God's property. The starting point in our theology of stewardship is to acknowledge that we are God's possession and not our own. On that solid foundation we can begin to build a value system that will determine the way we use our wealth throughout life. And that brings us to a liberating conclusion: *We can choose our standard of living*, which is discussed in the next chapter.

Chapter 2

Choosing Your Standard of Living

When I was a college student, I had a very hazy picture of my future life, but I assumed without question that my future would include an airplane. There was never a time during my childhood when my family didn't have a plane. I vividly remember throwing up in about as many family airplanes as family cars. I read the yellow tabloid pages of *Trade-a-Plane* every month as a teenager and debated the relative merits of Swifts and Luscombs. Even when Kathy and I were first married and I was in the air force, I assumed that we'd own an airplane at some point in our lives. Only when we responded to God's call to join the staff of Campus Crusade for Christ did I consciously face the fact that I would probably never earn enough money to afford a plane.

While most people may not feel they need to own an airplane, we all grow up with assumptions about our future lifestyles. We tend to expect that our standard of living will be similar to—or higher than—whatever we experienced in our parents' home. Another assumption is that our standard of living will be whatever our income can support. The idea of "choosing" to live at a particular level—especially a lower level than we actually earn—never crosses our minds.

Many young adults just out of college have a wonderful attitude toward living inexpensively. The tiny apartment, beat-up car, and meals of macaroni and cheese all seem to be a celebration of independent living rather than a hardship. However, as earning power increases, it becomes possible to make lifestyle upgrades, and the potential for making unwise choices increases dramatically.

The most fundamental issue in making wise and biblical choices about our lifestyle involves understanding exactly what the choices are. Let's take a look at the various options.

First, *we can spend more than we earn.* This is the most common choice Americans make today, but in past generations it was difficult. In biblical times, for example, people ate food purchased with whatever they earned that day. In other words, practically everyone was on a cash or barter basis. This remained true until the early 1950s, when widespread consumer credit became available. This financial revolution has made it possible for practically everyone to spend more than they make. The result is that it has become possible to have a luxurious lifestyle without actually having money. No longer do you need to be a millionaire to live like a millionaire! Through the miracle of easy credit you can live well today on what you *might* earn in the years or decades ahead.

I occasionally read net-worth surveys in *Money* magazine and the *Wall Street Journal* and am always shocked by the number of people who, after working for years, owe more than the net value of all their assets. In other words, if they sold everything they owned and applied the proceeds to their debts, they would still be in the hole!

You're probably thinking this is not a good option for a Christian. You're right, but I've known many Christians who are just as susceptible to the lure of credit as non-Christians are. Many people migrate into this category without intending to do so. It's so easy to spend a bit more than we have; we need only to say the simple phrase, "Just put it on this card, please." After a few months or years the resulting debt becomes a mountainous burden, a weight that can crush our lives for decades. (I'll talk more about how to tame the "debt monster" in chapter 18.)

Most of us, however, don't use credit to seek a luxurious lifestyle. The fact is, we find it quite easy to justify making purchases on credit. Often it's because we're just a bit short at the end of the pay period, so we charge the grocery bill. Or the baby has an ear infection and we charge the medicine. Or the front tires are bald and we put a new pair on the card. Even though we're not using credit to lease luxury cars or buy Patek Philippe watches, we are still borrowing from future earnings to buy what we can't afford today.

The comedian and sitcom star Tim Allen is famous for the idea that anything can be improved by adding *more power*. My own need for more power is most keenly felt in the arena of computer technology. I love to be near, if not actually on, the cutting edge. When my friends and associates upgrade their computers so that mine is no longer the fastest or has the most memory, biggest hard drive, or the latest Intel microprocessor, my subconscious immediately

begins to go to work. Every little problem with my current oper-
ating system is translated into an excuse to upgrade, swap, or expand.
It is tempting sometimes to upgrade on the easy terms offered by
my local computer superstore. However, by knowing my personal
tendencies, understanding the nature of the temptation, and rec-
ognizing that the computer I have is the computer God has given
me to use today, I defer upgrades until they are financially feasible
from my actual earnings.

The second lifestyle option available to us is not to spend more
than our income, but not to spend any less either. In other words,
we spend all of our income but not a penny more. This option keeps
us out of debt, but it also keeps us on the edge.

People in this category, which I'll call the "break-even" folks, are
typically much closer to the indebted category than they think.
When hiking in the mountains, I avoid walking close to the edge
of a cliff because I fear the consequences of accidentally stepping
over it. Likewise, just one financial mishap—losing a job, the car
breaking down, a trip to the emergency room—can send these
spenders over the edge. Because credit is available (thanks to Sir Visa
and Master Card), these break-eveners can charge the groceries, or
the repair, or the hospital bill. Good-bye to break-even, hello to debt!

The third option when choosing our lifestyle is to *spend less
than we earn*. This is the option I believe we should embrace. Think
about it: When we live this way, our income always exceeds our
expenses. Does this mean we must take a vow of poverty and go
about in rags, either begging for food or trusting God to deliver it
like manna from heaven? Not at all. It just means that making a
conscious decision to live within our income requires planning and

skills we may not have mastered, as well as an attitude and an approach to money management that most of us haven't cultivated.

This principle of spending less than we earn can apply to anyone, regardless of whether their income is small or large. Kathy and I have had the opportunity to become acquainted with Christians who are very wealthy—some who are worth tens of millions of dollars. Many of these individuals have decided that their income would not determine their standard of living, but that they would determine their standard of living and choose to give away all income above a certain threshold. For example, one individual I know gives away everything he earns over an income of $100,000.

Getting to rub shoulders with these mega-givers has given me the opportunity to observe the values that many of them share. One value that they adopted early in life is frugality: They chose to live comfortably within their income, especially when their income was low. The skills they acquired while managing a small income made it possible for them to effectively manage a large income. So don't despise a small income! There is great educational value in learning to live on a small income, and it is the best possible training for learning to live happily within a larger one if God provides it.

Most of us assume that a large infusion of cash would solve all our financial problems. Those who play the lottery or other get-rich-quick schemes dream that hitting the lucky jackpot will dramatically change their lives for the better. However, those who go quickly from rags to riches usually haven't developed the disciplines required to manage the money they already have, let alone a huge cash windfall. Unless a newly enriched individual engages a wise money manager, that "lucky" winner will probably be broke again in no time. Why? Because he thought he needed money, when what he really needed were good money-management skills.

Managing your resources involves skills that anybody can learn, but the most important aspects aren't technical; they're mostly a matter of attitude. With that in mind, let's turn now to the relationship between wealth and contentment.

Chapter 3

The Secret of Contentment

As I hung suspended by a nylon rope a hundred feet above the cavern floor, my legs cramping and the only light in my universe being the flame from my wavering carbide lamp, all I could think about was...crackers! Specifically, what kept me climbing foot by painful foot up that muddy rope from the cave below was the thought of the food I had left in a small pack at the top of that pit sixteen hours earlier.

Finally reaching the limestone ledge at the top of the pit, I threw myself on the soft dirt of the floor and frantically tore at the wrappings of cheese-and-cracker snack packs and bags of squashed cheese and mangled turkey slices. While I waited for the rest of my party to make the ascent, I lay in blissful luxury, savoring the crunch of cracker and the strips of turkey and cheese. Ah, what contentment! What sensual joy!

As I reflect on my cave-exploring days in college, I often wonder if food will ever again taste as wonderful as that did or if any bed will prove as inviting as the pebble-strewn floor of a cave. Why were those kitchen scraps so delicious? What magic made that rocky ground so comfortable?

It's clear that a great deal of our present happiness is rooted in our expectations, and not necessarily any particular level of comfort in which we find ourselves. Clearly the best part of my post-climb contentment was rooted in my perspective. Anything was better than freezing, cramping, and starving! I'm convinced that our expectations—whether met or unmet—are key to our contentment in most areas of life. Whenever our expectations exceed reality, we experience discontent.

But does simple contentment have to be so elusive? Can we learn the secret to turning off the tiny critic inside our psyches that constantly disparages what we have in order to extol the virtues of what we don't have? Perhaps not unless we have an experience that puts things into perspective.

In the summer of 1981 I learned what it was like to be wealthy. I had taken my family to the remote island country of Fiji in the South Pacific. I was in seminary at the time, and part of our goal as a family was to discover if we could adjust to living as missionaries in the so-called Third World. With our daughter, Laurie, being only five and our son, Josh, not quite three, Kathy was dubious about our ability to survive in what we were told might be a fairly primitive situation. Our fears were greatly allayed, however, when we arrived in Fiji. As our Fijian host drove us to our home for the summer, he said, "Don't worry; you'll be staying at my sister's place. It's a fully furnished house!"

We soon discovered that for a Fijian, a house is "fully furnished" when every room has a mat made of woven grass on the floor. Instead of a closet, a wire had been strung across a corner of the bedroom, complete with two empty coat hangers. We found out later the reason for the two coat hangers: The owner had only two shirts!

We were fairly taken aback at our "fully furnished" home, and Josh loudly announced there was no way he would stay. Fortunately, our hosts couldn't understand Josh, and he (and we) did stay. During that summer we made a wonderful adjustment to the simplicity of Third-World life. We slept on the mats in the bedroom and ate on the mat in the kitchen. And every morning Laurie and Josh swept out dead insects using a straw broom made by our Hindu next-door neighbors.

During that summer we came to know many Fijians, most of whom lived on monthly incomes equivalent to what we paid for a month's electricity back in California. Yet they demonstrated vast contentment. They had discovered that contentment had nothing to do with how much they had but was a by-product of being thankful for God's blessings.

My wealth didn't increase a dime that summer, but compared to the average Fijian, I was richer than Bill Gates! And I learned a lot about what I believe the apostle Paul was trying to communicate when he wrote in Philippians 4:12: "I know what it is to be in need, and I know what it is to have plenty. I have learned the secret of being content in any and every situation, whether well fed or hungry, whether living in plenty or in want."

Paul is perhaps one of the greatest biblical examples of a person who really understood the significance of wealth in a Christian's life. Regardless of whether he was living humbly or overflowing with goodies, Paul was content. But his contented attitude didn't just happen—he had to learn it!

Why does this seem so difficult for us today? To answer that question, let's take a brief historical detour. At the beginning of the twenty-first century, we are the heirs of a great river of cultural influence that had its headwaters in the Renaissance, and to understand that influence, we need to go all the way back to the medieval world. It's difficult for us to understand the world-view that dominated the Western world prior to the Renaissance—a view that held that everything worth knowing was already known, that everything possible had already been invented. Progress was not only inconceivable but, if advocated, was met with suspicion and hostility.

Sometime after the fourteenth century, this medieval mind-set was replaced with a great cultural reorientation called the Renaissance. The Renaissance brought with it the belief that progress was possible and even desirable. Society became convinced that broken things could be fixed (leading to the Reformation, among other things). This stream gathered momentum as the Industrial Revolution began in the eighteenth century, and then it overflowed into the first great century of innovation and invention—the nineteenth.

The watchword of the new age was "progress," and nowhere was this mantra chanted with more devotion than in America. Great engineers like Thomas Edison, George Westinghouse, Samuel Morse, Alexander Graham Bell, and Henry Ford brought marvels of technology within the reach of the common man, and the common man began to experience an unprecedented economic boom. Even humble working people were able to buy clocks, dishes, cars, refrigerators, radios—you name it. Our century has seen an almost unbroken trend of rising wages and rising expectations. The only exception was the Great Depression of the 1930s, possibly rendered even more painful by the universal expectation of continual progress.

My point is that our mind-set in the new millennium is the opposite of the medieval mind-set. Where the concept of progress was almost inconceivable to the people who lived then, a lack of progress is unthinkable to us. We believe that standards of living must rise, that cars must become more luxurious, and that computer systems must become more efficient. We have, in short, a built-in cultural prejudice against the concept of contentment with what we have and are therefore programmed to be dissatisfied with our current resources.

How then can we understand Paul being content "whether living in plenty or in want"? Let me take a swing at defining *contentment* as living joyfully on God's provision. It's short and sweet, isn't it? Note that it doesn't depend on the *quantity* of God's provision. Whether we have a lot or a little, the point is that God has provided. We see that Paul's life had periods of "abundant" provision contrasted with times of great hardship, such as being unjustly beaten and chained in vermin-infested jails (Acts 16). Yet Paul demonstrated his contentment even here by singing songs of praise to God!

Contentment, then, has no direct relationship to our wealth, except that we are to rejoice in whatever wealth God has given us. Our cultural programming tells us, "But it's easier to rejoice with greater wealth than with less!" Actually, that's probably not true.

Increasing wealth tends to increase our cares, not our joy. If we can't learn to live joyfully with our present wealth, then increasing wealth isn't likely to change our attitude.

Almost thirty years ago, as a newly minted second lieutenant in the air force, I found myself earning a much smaller paycheck than most of my fellow college graduates who did not find themselves in the military as a result of drawing an absurdly low number in the national draft lottery. On the other hand, compared to the enlisted men and women at my little radar site, the paycheck Kathy and I cashed twice a month was truly princely, a huge salary received mostly for supervising the real workers.

As we came to the end of my military term, we were faced with a crucial decision. On the one hand, we were enormously attracted to Christian ministry with Campus Crusade for Christ. On the other, many wanted us to join a family business. If we chose the ministry option, our salary not only wouldn't increase from the military level, but it would take an abrupt dive. If we chose to join the family business, our income would jump enormously.

Although we had a lot yet to learn about contentment, we were convinced that if we placed ourselves in the center of God's will, then whatever income was provided would certainly be enough to live on with godly satisfaction. We believed God was calling us into full-time ministry, so to the surprise of many of our friends, we declined the lucrative family business opportunity.

We haven't regretted that choice. While we have found our income over the years to be much smaller than that of our college friends, it is far greater than that of people in Third-World countries. Our Fijian experience taught us much about cultivating contentment.

As Paul wrote near the end of his life, "But godliness with contentment is great gain" (1 Timothy 6:6). Like Paul and like our Fijian friends, we had begun to *learn* to be content, and that's an investment that continues to pay dividends.

Not everybody can be a financial Einstein, but each of us can cultivate the attitude of contentment. When we practice contentment, we needn't have the latest, greatest, or most expensive, but whatever our circumstances we will learn to say to ourselves, "It doesn't get any better than this!"

Chapter 4

The ABCs of Money Management

I believe that what distinguished Kathy and me from countless young couples just starting out was that we got some excellent advice on finance in the first weeks of our marriage and immediately began to implement it.

I met my wife-to-be when we were students at Duke University in Durham, North Carolina, on a Campus Crusade Halloween hayride. We married the year she graduated, a year I had spent getting advanced training in managing air force radar systems. When we settled down on the central coast of California, we began to look for a place to worship and eventually found a church home in San Luis Obispo.

We dropped by on a Saturday and found the church abuzz with volunteers who were scrubbing, weeding, and painting. One paint-spattered individual turned out to be the pastor, Johnny Boswell, a jovial ex-ballplayer who gave us a warm welcome. When he found out we were newlyweds, he beamed at us and told us he would give us the best financial advice he had ever received, when he and his wife were married. He said, "Ray and Kathy, you just can't do better in your lives than to make this commitment right from the beginning: *Give some, save some, and live joyfully on the rest.*"

I'm not sure why that simple piece of advice made such a strong impression on us. Perhaps it was the sense that Pastor Boswell was offering a principle of great worth, something like an heirloom that is passed from generation to generation. Whatever the reason, we resolved to live according to its wisdom. We'd observed enough marriages to know that many couples find finances a source of strain and conflict, even misery. And some individuals start making poor choices early in adult life that weigh them down for years and cripple their ability to live joyfully on the bounty God provides. We didn't want to fall into those familiar traps.

I'll never forget a couple we met shortly after we were married. The Millers had three children and a fourth on the way. We gathered often at their home for Bible studies and came to know well their beat-up sofa, scarred coffee and end tables, and decrepit easy chair. We initially thought that all this furniture had been scrounged at the local Goodwill store. But, in fact, the furniture was less than five years old and had been bought new on a time-payment plan that was still running. I can't tell you what an impression this made on us. The Millers were paying a good deal of money every month for what amounted to garage-sale junk!

While attitude is the single most important key to "living large," even on a little, most of us also need practical training in resource management. We need to balance our attitude (contentment with what we have) with hands-on skills in managing our resources (mostly money, time, and things) with greater effectiveness. Except for that class in the tenth grade that taught us how to balance a checkbook (a skill that escaped me for another decade), too few of us have been prepared to manage our finances, even on an elementary level.

The rest of this book is my attempt to pass on more of the details of what I've learned and practiced in the realm of personal resource management for the past three decades. The next section covers the biblical underpinnings and practical how-tos related to that first element in our pastor's "formula" for a happy marriage and successful adulthood: *giving*. I have discovered that giving can be one of a Christian's greatest joys, and that Scripture offers several principles that can serve as a foundation for our attitude and practice of sharing our resources with others. I pray that you will experience the joy and adventure Kathy and I have as we've learned to give our time and money cheerfully, generously, expectantly, strategically, and systematically.

The third section of this book explores important principles related to the second element of Johnny Boswell's advice: *saving*. Most of us have not received much practical advice on how to take the first steps in building a cushion to soften the day-to-day financial blows that tempt us to take on debt. I'll introduce you to some basic ideas that can get you started down the road of avoiding debt and building assets. I'll also sketch out the pitfalls of accumulating wealth and encourage you to resist trusting in your nest egg rather than in God.

Finally, the last section will walk you through the many aspects of our pastor's third piece of advice: *live joyfully on the rest*. This is what some people would deem the fun part of money management—spending it!

I am so grateful for Pastor Johnny and his advice to Kathy and me, and I hope that this book will help many others to avoid the snares set for the unwary in the financial woods. Even if you've already made financial mistakes, you can learn how to recover.

When Kathy and I had been married about ten years, had bought a house, and had acquired significant savings, we became intrigued by an ad in our local newspaper. A company called Universal Financial Services was offering very high interest rates to depositors. We checked on the company with the Better Business Bureau—they had no complaints on record. We went to the UFS offices and spoke to a representative. He assured us that our deposits with the company were secured by the properties on which the company made mortgage loans to borrowers. In every respect the company seemed to be on the level, so we ultimately invested most of our savings with them.

Oops. The company was a scam. Its "administrators" made interest payments to prior investors out of money entrusted to them by "investors" like us. It was a "Ponzi scheme," and in only a few months our local headlines were screaming about the fraud and deception at Universal Financial. Ultimately, the CEO went to jail for a few years, but millions in assets were never recovered. We lost, figuratively speaking, our shirts.

I'll admit this was a blow. But we chose to thank God that he was still in control of our money, our lives, and the universe in general. Then we thanked him for the reminder that we should never wear the cloak of "ownership" too tightly. We never got our money back, and while I fantasized about how I would exact my revenge from that crooked CEO (ways involving acid, spiders, electric shock—and yes, I should be ashamed!), God miraculously met our needs and restored our financial health in a thousand subtle ways.

Truly, it's never too late to begin to live large, even on a little. Take it from me. Now let's dive into the bottomless ocean of God's wealth and discover the foundation on which it is all constructed: giving, God's way.

SECTION 2

THE JOY OF GIVING

❖

Chapter 5

God Loves a Cheerful Giver

Ever since my son, Josh, was a child, he had a special sympathy for the poor and homeless. I particularly remember one occasion when we were trying to teach him the importance of budgeting his money and so gave him an entire month's allowance all at once. A few days later, while getting gas near downtown, Josh noticed a grimy and unshaven individual holding a sign reading, "Will work for food." Josh walked over and happily gave the homeless man a five-dollar bill—half of his entire allowance.

My first reaction was hardly positive. We had just given Josh that money, and he had given it away. Our son had, in effect, given *our* money to that homeless person. Only on reflection did I realize that Josh had perfectly modeled the most basic principle of Christian giving—that when we give, it is not our resources, but God's, that we share. No wonder Josh gave away his allowance so happily—it was his father's money, and there was more where that came from!

Now contrast my son's spirit of generosity with my own actions at the same age. One of my vivid memories of fourth grade was a Christmas party during which my classmates and I exchanged gifts. Everyone brought a wrapped gift, and since my last name began with "A," I got to pick from the pile first. When Johnny Wilson's turn finally came up, the gifts were all gone. Consternation ruled. Who had not brought a gift? How could this happen? What shall we do now? I was sitting next to my teacher, so I leaned over and whispered, "He can have mine."

The dilemma suddenly solved, I experienced a brief moment of selfless generosity before being engulfed in my teacher's arms. Almost weeping, she promised to reward my act with virtually anything my heart desired. I was a hero. Why? Because I had briefly practiced the timeworn adage, "It is better to give than to receive."

In this particular case I had come out doubly blessed, for my teacher had never realized that my surreptitious gropings through the wrapping paper had told me that the toy I had selected was one of those "educational" toys that required one to move wooden letters around a track in order to spell different words. I was actually glad to unload it, and Johnny Wilson was not exactly thrilled to receive it. However, the principle—that it's better to give than receive—still holds, despite my flawed motives!

The principle that my son, Josh, so naturally followed is what the apostle Paul described in 2 Corinthians 9:7: "Each man should give what he has decided in his heart to give, not reluctantly or under compulsion, for God loves a cheerful giver." This verse makes it clear that giving is to be an individual (or couple) responsibility, and it is not something that can be arbitrarily imposed by another.

Only the people involved can be sure that they are giving at a level that is free ("not under compulsion") and such that, after the gift is made, they can rejoice in having given it. As Christians, our giving is to be governed by grace, not controlled by some misplaced legalism.

I have experienced giving to be one of the great delights of life. It gives joy to the giver, and it brings happiness to the recipient. Generous giving should characterize every aspect of the Christian life. Jesus advised his disciples before he sent them on the ministry trip recorded in Matthew 10:8, "Freely you have received, freely give." Because Christ freely gave his life for us, we should be generous in our giving.

Always remember that God has infinite resources, and that which we give as his children is not ours, but his. If Christ is really Lord of all, then he will be Lord of our checkbook and Day-Timer as well! Our giving validates to whom we really belong—to ourselves, or to the Lord. When we are willing to give freely, out of recognition that we are God's possession, then we are offering to the world a powerful testimony of our transformed nature and our Father's generosity. If we aren't willing to give freely, then we are contradicting what we say about our new nature in Christ.

For who do we say that we are in Christ? Don't we say that we have become "born again," joint heirs with Christ of all of God's riches? If we say this is true about us—and it is—by virtue of our adoption into God's family, then isn't it just a teeny bit inconsistent to be tight-fisted with our giving? Why should we be stingy about sharing God's resources? The Christian who says, "My Heavenly Father owns it all—but I'm not giving you anything!" is clearly sending out mixed messages, and it is his deeds that will be believed, not his words.

Josh instinctively understood this when he gave away half of his resources. If he had given it all, would we have "punished" him for that? Hardly! In reality, we were delighted by his spirit of generosity and wanted to cultivate in ourselves the kind of open-handedness that should characterize those whose heavenly Father really does own the cattle on a thousand hills. Why not give cheerfully, happily, even hilariously? It's not ours, we can't keep it, and—there's more where that came from!

Chapter 6

Time: Your Most Valuable Asset

On a recent trip to Russia I was fortunate to have the opportunity to see a number of jeweled Easter eggs made for the Russian czar and his family by the greatest goldsmith who ever lived, Carl Gustavovich Fabergé. The security at the Hermitage museum in Saint Petersburg was extraordinary, and I learned that on the rare occasions that Fabergé eggs were available at auction, they invariably sold for many millions of dollars.

What made a few ounces of gold and precious stones so valuable? It wasn't just the raw materials. I estimated the value of the gold and jewels in such a treasure at only a few percent of the market price of a Fabergé egg. While some eggs contained ingenious clockwork mechanisms of great elegance and complexity, neither did this account for their great value. When I considered other art treasures—such as Michelangelo's *David* or Leonardo da Vinci's *Mona Lisa*—the value of the raw materials was almost nothing in comparison with the worth of the finished works of art.

I believe that everything tangible that is valued in human society can ultimately be traced back to the time it took (or takes) to find, develop, organize, design, create, or anything else that people do to things that increases their value. What makes the autograph of a famous athlete valuable? Anybody can sign his name on a baseball, but that doesn't increase the baseball's value. The value of an autographed baseball doesn't reflect the few seconds it took for the athlete to write his name, but rather the time and effort he expended in becoming one of the best in the world.

After my tour through the museum, I sat sipping tea in the snack bar and reflected on what is most valuable of all. If I was being robbed at gunpoint in a dark alley, and the robber was foolish enough to accept my change purse and Russian watch, I would count myself lucky. If he demanded more, I would with increasing reluctance hand over first my wallet, then my keys, and finally my wedding ring. I would willingly give up all material assets to retain my life, so clearly life is more valuable than things.

Time is life itself, and in this life it is far more precious than any tangible object. But time is seldom recognized as "wealth," or in the same category as precious metals, stocks, real estate, etc. You would never see in a net-worth statement a line-entry for an asset labeled "Remaining Time on Earth: not known." As Christians, however, I believe this is exactly the way we should view the most valuable asset God has given us. Our real wealth is not cash or assets—our money and tangible possessions—it is our time. It is time that gives us the potential to make changes of eternal significance, as well as the means to make exchanges in the market-place. For example, we can trade our labor (time spent doing work) into wages for cash. With this cash we can make more trades. We can trade it for things (cars, soap, fertilizer), other labor (mechanics to fix the car, gardeners to cut the grass), or even, sometimes, more time (medical procedures to prolong life).

This lengthy explanation has a point, and here it is: As stewards of God's property, we would be pretty foolish to carefully guard the many trinkets he has entrusted to us and yet mindlessly squander the few things that are really valuable! That was the point of Jesus' criticism of the Pharisees who were meticulous in tithing their herbs from their gardens, yet cared nothing for values such as justice and compassion. If our life belongs to God, and our time is merely the expression of our life in action, then our time belongs to God. Since our time is convertible to other things, like cash, then we need to treat our time with as much respect as we would the most valuable material asset.

When I was in the midst of my seminary education, I met a wonderful couple whose son became good friends with Josh. These people had labored for many years in the Philippines, and I grew very appreciative of the creativity and intensity of their ministry. I wondered at what point they would ask us to help them financially in their ministry in that country. Even before they asked, Kathy and I were willing to pull out our checkbook and make our first donation.

To my amazement, however, they didn't ask for money. Instead, they asked us to go to Asia and minister in their place! Years before I had spent several anxious years in the air force awaiting a transfer to Vietnam that never came, and the word "Asia" called to mind a continent teeming with poverty, wretchedness, and disease. Now this missionary wanted me to move (with my wife and two young children!) to this continent of misery.

God led Kathy and me through a long and educational journey before both of us yielded to the fact that he was, indeed, calling us to minister in Asia. And far from being a sink of suffering, we found Asia full of delightful people, amazing cultures, and many individuals thirsting for the grace of God available through Christ. But the chief lesson we learned is that it is far easier to give our money than our time, because time is life. When we were ready to yield our time back to God, then he could be sure our lives were fully his.

If the core principle in the Christian management of wealth is that God owns us as well as all of our possessions, then giving our time (e.g., ourselves), more than anything else, is a way of demonstrating his ownership of us. If we're willing to give our money, but not our time, then we prove that we're still attempting to own what actually belongs to God.

After all, what am I but God's "Fabergé egg"? He made me from a few cents' worth of raw materials, yet he poured into me his time, his creativity, his genius for design in order to fashion me as a unique individual and his private property. Every moment that he gives me, I'm faced with the choice to affirm God's ownership of me (my time and my money) or to deny his ownership by affirming it for myself.

I have learned over many years that when I yield to God's absolute Lordship in my life, I experience delight and joy and divine surprises. Now when I yield my time and my material assets to him, I *expect* God to use my giving in extraordinary ways. My expectations seldom go unmet, as we will see in the next chapter.

Chapter 7

Give Expectantly

The process of entering a strange country is always interesting and sometimes very confusing for the newcomer. When I was coming through customs at the Borispol Airport in Kiev, Ukraine, I encountered a perfectly baffled Japanese gentleman who had spent several hours trying to discover how to escape from the purgatory of the customs arrival hall. It seems that he needed to fill out a customs declaration form, but there were no forms available. Since I knew where to find the blank forms, I gave him a supply and showed him how to fill them out correctly. His joy and gratitude knew no bounds. He wanted to reward me, but how could I take anything from him when I had simply given to him what had been freely given to me? Besides, I had gained great satisfaction from helping him.

This illustrates a basic biblical principle: God intends for us not only to give cheerfully and generously, but also to gain great satisfaction and blessing from our giving. Jesus said in his Sermon on the Mount: "Give, and it will be given to you. A good measure, pressed down, shaken together and running over, will be poured into your lap. For with the measure you use, it will be measured to you" (Luke 6:38).

Was Jesus giving his listeners a "break-even" giving strategy? Was he encouraging us to be motivated in our giving by the expectation that he'll "pay us back" according to our sacrifice? Some believers put just this kind of strange twist on the principle of giving in faith, rightly expecting God to respond.

For example, I once listened to a speaker who implied that the real motivation to give was so that we might receive. He illustrated it like this: "Do you want to REAP twenty-dollar bills? Then you've got to PLANT twenty-dollar bills! Do you want to reap HUNDRED-dollar bills? Then you've got to PLANT hundred-dollar bills!" He went on to assert that "God doesn't want his children to be poor." He maintained that as a result of following his own advice, "I wear a thousand-dollar suit! I eat steak every day!" He claimed that the sowing-reaping mechanism is built into the universe as God's way of guaranteeing that the believer who sows abundantly will surely become rich.

Such a reading of the scripture is based on the false understanding that what we have belongs to us, not to the Lord: If we give up some of "ours," then God will give us back even more, which then becomes "ours." This violates the foundational concept that it *all* belongs to the Lord, even if he lets us use it.

Scripture does teach, however, that God multiplies the resources we give in his name, and because of this we can expect wonderful "returns" as a result of our giving. Paul reiterates this principle in 2 Corinthians 9:6: "Remember this: Whoever sows sparingly will also reap sparingly, and whoever sows generously will also reap generously." Paul was explaining the paradoxical idea that what we give away does not decrease what we have left but actually increases it.

On the surface, this flies in the face of common sense. "Billie has forty-seven cents. If he spends twelve cents on an ice cream cone, how much does Billie have left?" Obviously Billie has thirty-five cents left of "his" money. But let's change the equation a bit: "Janie was entrusted with forty-seven cents of God's money. Janie gives twelve cents to help a fellow Christian in need. How much money does God have left?"

God's resources are indeed infinite, yet he is willing to entrust some of them to us. But how can we know whether or not he is willing to trust us with more? The answer is simple: If you look upon the money as "yours," you don't get more. If you treat it as "his," demonstrating this by being willing to give it, then he is willing to trust you with more, even up into the millions.

Paul used a farming metaphor to illustrate God's ability to multiply resources:

"Now he who supplies seed to the sower and bread for food will also supply and increase your store of seed and will enlarge the harvest of your righteousness. You will be made rich in every way so that you can be generous on every occasion, and through us your generosity will result in thanksgiving to God" (2 Corinthians 9:10-11).

It is God who provides seed, and it is God who multiplies the seed sown. So if God does all the hard work, what is left for the farmer? His job is simple: to take some perfectly good seed—seed that could be made into flour then bread or bagels or lemon-filled tarts—and plant it in the ground. In other words, to waste it, ruin it, and bury it. The amazing outcome of all of this is that the buried seed is reborn many times over, and provides not only seed for the next sowing season, but food aplenty for the farmer and others.

Just as a farmer looks eagerly for the first shoots of his new crop to appear, we should give expectantly, anticipating the first signs of a new "crop." How does this work in practice? Almost exactly as with the farmer. We write a check and give. Or we spend two weeks on a short-term mission. Or we prepare for and teach a Sunday school class. But now we need to keep our eyes open—how is God going to give back to us?

A young married couple, still students, who were a part of our campus ministry at Ball State University, grasped this concept early in their marriage. They were facing a severe financial crunch. They didn't have the resources for the next quarter's tuition, and we wanted them to attend a student-leadership conference to get more advanced training in student ministry. As they prayed about the situation, they felt led to take some of their dwindling cash—not enough for their own conference expenses—and use it to provide a scholarship for another student to the conference. They then asked God to meet their own needs, although they couldn't imagine how this could happen. The next week they reported to us, joyfully wide-eyed, that God had amazingly provided not only for their next quarter's tuition, but enough for their own conference expenses!

Paul assures us that the "seed" we plant into the lives of others bears many kinds of fruit. Not only does God often return additional "seed money" to us, but the gift itself does many good things along the way. Needs are met, the church is built up, and it all results in thanksgiving to God!

Through giving, then, many things are simultaneously accomplished, but most importantly we demonstrate that we don't own the "seed," but God does. Note that nowhere in this theology of giving are we "giving back to God." God doesn't need anything given back! God's plan is that we share his resources so that the whole body of Christ will have its needs supplied. As we share the resources God has entrusted to us, Paul assures us that "God is able to make all grace abound to you, so that in all things at all times, having all that you need, you will abound in every good work" (2 Corinthians 9:8).

Think about that: abounding grace in all things at all times. Sounds pretty good, doesn't it? And the key is being loose-fisted with what isn't ours in the first place, but God's.

But how loose-fisted should we be? And with whom should we be sharing our resources? Are there strategies for giving that make the very best use of God's resources toward the goals of his kingdom here on earth? These are some of the questions we'll explore next.

Chapter 8

Give Strategically

Once I had a dream—or was it a nightmare? I dreamed that it was 1976, and I had just met a young hippie named Steve Jobs. "Ray, I've got this great idea for a computer we're going to call the Apple. But I need start-up capital! What do you say about putting up $5,000 to get things rolling, and I'll give you 10 percent of the company?" The dream turns into a nightmare when I blow him off— "No way, you long-haired loser!"

Outstanding investment opportunities are always easy to pick when we have the clarity of hindsight. Sometimes making strategic investments in God's kingdom through giving is just as tough as picking financial investments in the business world. Out of all the countless appeals for donations that we receive in the course of a year (or month or week), how can we possibly select the most worthy? How can we sort the wheat from the bulk-mail chaff that comes our way?

I know a godly individual who periodically gets so overwhelmed with fund-raising appeals that he becomes paralyzed, unable to give at all until a personal appeal from someone he knows and trusts breaks the logjam. I can just hear him now—"They all sound so good, so worthy, so needy. I just can't choose between them!" Interestingly, he is an astute financial investor and has no difficulty sifting the so-so corporations from the likely winners.

Of course, one of our first giving targets should be our local church. That choice is a no-brainer, but we can also give far beyond the needs of our own church.

When selecting the people and organizations with whom you share your resources, my advice is to follow a strategy similar to one you'd use to identify corporate winners. When I consider what kind of company in which I'd like to invest, I look for a well-managed corporation run by men and women of vision and integrity with a top-notch product that customers are lining up to buy. Once I identify a company like this, I know that, barring the unexpected, it's going to make money for its investors.

When applying a similar criteria to selecting targets for strategic giving, I consider the same issues. Is the organization managed well by men and women of integrity? I apply an immediate filter to virtually all fund appeals, which is this: Does the organization belong to the Evangelical Council for Financial Accountability? This is a voluntary association of mission and ministry agencies that have set very high standards for maintaining financial integrity in their organizations. You can be sure that funds given to ECFA members will not wind up in some con artist's collection of Rolls-Royces.

While the ECFA ensures high standards of financial integrity, it is also important that the organization itself be efficiently managed. This is more difficult for an outsider to evaluate, but some of the signs of a well-managed organization should be obvious. Do they issue receipts for your gifts promptly and correctly? Are their staff members well-trained, motivated, and focused on the objective of their mission? Have they become distracted from their core mission and focused instead on building a top-heavy administrative structure?

Personally, I am intent on putting gifts to the work of God's kingdom into shoe leather and am not as keen on constructing buildings or upgrading computer systems, although I recognize the importance of these items. Kathy and I are not personally excited about supporting missions that are not involved in directly helping to expand God's kingdom, as worthwhile as some of these organizations are in terms of their humanitarian efforts. We want the portion of God's money with which we've been entrusted to be active on the front lines, spreading the gospel.

However, just as not everybody has the same gifts, abilities, and callings, so not everybody is led to give with equal enthusiasm to every good cause. When we look at Jesus' earthly ministry, we see that he healed, delivered from demons, and fed the multitudes. The apostle Paul wrote, "Therefore, as we have opportunity, let us do good to all people, especially to those who belong to the family of believers" (Galatians 6:10). While I rejoice in primarily evangelistic ministries, others are called to primarily humanitarian causes. God clearly calls his children to be involved in relieving hunger, homelessness, and despair. Ideally, such humanitarian aid would point the physically and emotionally needy to the One who can meet all their needs, including spiritual needs. Bottom line: Whatever causes God calls you to support with his resources, give to them heartily to the glory of God!

Another aspect of giving strategically has to do with Uncle Sam. We are privileged, as Americans, to live in a country that values charitable contributions, even ones aimed at evangelism and discipleship. A contribution given to a charity that meets all relevant IRS standards—sometimes known as a 501c(3) organization—qualifies as an adjustment to the taxpayer's adjusted gross income. In my travels I have not found a single foreign government that gives taxpayers a break on charitable contributions. The gracious aspects of the U.S. tax system make it possible to give a great deal more than we might otherwise suspect we can, especially if we give a gift of stock rather than cash.

Here's how it works. As you wisely invest a portion of your resources (we'll talk all about saving and investing in the next section), you may select some Olympic-class investment performers along the way. If you paid $500 for a block of XYZ Corporation and it has proven incredibly successful for the past ten years, then it may now be worth $20,000 or more. This gives you both a problem and a great opportunity.

The problem is that if you should liquidate that stock into cash, you would have to pay capital gains tax on it! Bummer! The opportunity is that if you just give the stock itself to a qualified charity, you get an income tax deduction—not of your initial $500 investment, but of the full $20,000 value. And this applies whether or not your income tax bracket is low or high. In fact, it is possible to give so much by giving appreciated stock that you may have to carry over some of that deduction into the next year's taxes.

Such a deal: a great giving opportunity and reduced taxes for dessert! This is the greatest of win-win situations when it comes to using God's resources wisely and strategically. Your gift blesses the recipient and nets you a tax savings at the same time. In fact, this opportunity is so great that it creates yet another problem, but this is a minor one that is easily solved.

Let's say you don't want to give the whole block of stock to just one organization, or perhaps you would like to give some now, some in a few months, and more later. It would be simple if you could sell the stock and just distribute money, but if you do that you will wreck the whole opportunity to avoid income tax on your gains. Don't do it! Instead, give the block of stock to an intermediary, such as the Fidelity Charitable Gift Fund. They are a bona fide 501c(3) charitable institution that exists for one purpose: to funnel blocks of stock to designated charities.

Here's how to use such a fund to give strategically. First, transfer the shares of XYZ stock to the charitable gift fund. They will then send you the appropriate form to use at tax time as proof of your donation. The fund will sell your stock and put the net assets into an account invested in conservative stocks. You then direct the fund to make disbursements from that account to the charities you've identified as good targets for your giving. The result is that you make the gift, take the deduction, then direct disbursements to qualifying charities until the money is gone. It's a marvelous system and could be wisely used by many who make cash gifts when a gift of appreciated stock could have a much greater impact for God's kingdom.

While God has always had enough assets—metals, foodstuff, real estate—to fund the expansion of his kingdom, he honors us with the privilege of being his intermediaries. Are we willing to echo the young Isaiah: "Here am I—send me!"? God wants our hearts far more than he needs our money! But once he has our hearts, there are still some practical questions about giving: How much should we give? Where does generous giving turn into excessive giving? Is it possible to give beyond God's will for us? The next chapter will tackle those dilemmas.

How Much Should You Give?

I'll admit it: I tend to faint at the sight of blood—especially my own. Once I sliced the end of my left forefinger in a machine-shop accident, and I fainted three times before finally getting it bandaged up. I used to dread the USAF blood drives, because as an officer I would be expected to set the example in offloading my most precious bodily fluid.

Many Christians seem to believe that giving financially should be like my approach to giving blood: It doesn't count unless it makes you ill. I have often heard well-meaning Christians affirm that giving should be *sacrificial*. "If you haven't given until it hurts," some say, "then you haven't given at all! After all, Christ endured a great deal of pain in order to freely give us his righteousness, etc."

How does this truth relate to giving generously and cheerfully? I don't believe that "giving sacrificially" means "giving till it hurts." Giving should not necessarily be painful, even if it means giving all that we have. The concept of "painful giving" is not one that I see documented in scripture. While athletes are often expected to play through the pain, giving generously needn't be like playing football with a sprained ankle. I know that God gives generously to me, and I want to give generously to others. But why shouldn't I do whatever I can to increase my joy and contentment in giving? I know myself well enough to realize that I do the things I like and avoid the things I hate.

On the other hand, if by "sacrificial" one means "dedicated to the Lord," then I am entirely in favor of it. Just as the various sacrifices involved in worship at the temple were dedicated to the Lord, and just as Paul counseled the Romans to be "living sacrifices" (Romans 12:1-2), so our lives and our gifts should be dedicated wholly to God. This kind of sacrificial giving is excellent and is based solidly on the key truth that God owns us and, as we walk in the center of his will, we will freely distribute his assets as he leads us.

But what's the bottom line? you may still be wondering. *How much of what I make should I give away?* There is no universal standard in giving, any more than in any other aspect of the Christian life. By that I mean that we have freedom in giving, and there is no amount that can be predetermined in advance of the opportunity to give. "But what about the traditional tithe of 10 percent?" you might ask. "Isn't that the benchmark Christians are supposed to use?"

As a young Christian I heard over and over again about the Christian's obligation to "tithe" a certain percentage of his or her income. Tithing, many preachers said, was based on the Old Testament requirements of the Mosaic Law. It wasn't clear to me exactly why modern Christians were expected to tithe but not required to keep other requirements of the Law of Moses, such as avoiding pork. As I came to understand the Bible better, I found much that was good about the emphasis on tithing, but I have trouble with how the concept is often taught. Are we Christians supposed to tithe, to give a tenth of our income back to God and specifically to the local church?

I have decided that tithing is not well supported by the New Testament. Now don't get me wrong—the idea of *giving* is hugely promoted in the New Testament, and I'm entirely in favor of it. My problem is with *tithing* from both a biblical and practical perspective.

First, the biblical perspective. Much of the contemporary emphasis on tithing is based on a misunderstanding of the relationship between the Law of Moses and the modern Christian. The problem is that a specific requirement of the Mosaic Law has somehow been transmuted into an eternal principle. The Israelites and their descendants were in fact bound to give a tithe of this and a tithe of that, but the demands of the Mosaic Law are not binding on me as a Christian today. They are only illustrative of my responsibility to fulfill the new covenant of Christ in the power of the Holy Spirit.

Proponents of tithing in the church age can point to several biblical events to counter my objection. They observe that, in Genesis 14, Abraham gave a tithe to the priest Melchizedek after Abraham rescued his kinsmen. Since Abraham gave a tithe before the Mosaic covenant existed, runs this argument, then tithing is a principle for all ages.

This example proves an excellent point: *Giving* is a principle for all ages. It says nothing about the practice of tithing as it is usually understood. Let's examine what actually happened when

Abraham tithed to Melchizedek. What Abraham in fact did was give Melchizedek a tenth of the loot he recovered when he rescued his relatives from their abductors. There is not even a hint that Abraham consistently gifted Melchizedek with a tenth of his income, and that's the essence of tithing.

Another argument that tithing is an eternal principle is that Jesus presumably tithed and even commended his enemies for doing so. In Luke 11:42 Jesus noted that the Pharisees tithed from the increase of their herb gardens, saying, "You should have practiced the latter without leaving the former undone." So, this argument says, if Jesus approved of tithing and praised the Pharisees for doing so, then we should tithe as they did.

The flaw with this argument is that Jesus and the Pharisees were Jews and therefore under the Mosaic Law. Where in the book of Acts or the letters of Paul, Peter, John, or elsewhere do we see non-Jews burdened with any aspect of the Law? When the Jerusalem Council wrestled with whether or not the requirements of Judaism were to be imposed on believing Gentiles (Acts 15), the decision of the council affirmed that non-Jews were under no obligation to keep any part of the Mosaic Law.

So why is tithing taught so vigorously in many branches of the modern church? Perhaps because some have not actually examined the biblical background on tithing and have uncritically adopted and passed along what they have heard and been taught. And obviously those whose income depends on Christian giving have a vested interest in people continuing to tithe!

When Paul encouraged the Corinthians to give out of the goodness of their hearts, and "not under compulsion," he was calling them to a grace-based rather than legalistic kind of giving. Paul had just reminded the Corinthians that while they had committed themselves to a financial gift to meet the needs of Christians suffering from a famine in Jerusalem (see 2 Corinthians 9:1-5), they had not yet made the gift. Yet Paul wanted the Corinthians to complete their gift of their own free will. Paul wasn't negating the timeless principles and guidelines from God spelled out in the Mosaic Law, but he was making it clear that God prefers our free-will love offering to perpetual hoop-jumping sacrifices. Our new position in Christ under the new covenant provides us with a much greater sense of God's grace, and as a result we should have an inner motivation to want to give not just a small, technically calculated portion of what we possess, but rather give far more generously and freely.

That brings me to one result I see of unbiblical teaching on tithing: I believe that tithing the standard 10 percent is sometimes too limiting. Perhaps we should give even more, much more! We must not assume that just because we're giving a tenth (if we are), we've reached the highest level of Christian giving.

Second, on the practical side, many who are committed to tithing do so from wrong motives and therefore miss most of the benefits of giving. As I've already discussed, it is unbiblical to teach that if we give God "his" portion, then the rest is ours. This completely contradicts the fundamental concept of stewardship—that we are not our own property but belong to God. Remember: Christian management of wealth begins with a recognition that we ourselves, our time, our labor, and our possessions are actually the property of the Lord. Tithing, as it is often misunderstood, asserts our ownership of 90 percent of the wealth entrusted to us.

Have I been too hard on those who teach tithing? My objections are rooted in the fact that it is too limiting for us in the modern age. In building a house, the contractor must first prepare the ground and correctly lay the foundation. In the same way, Christian giving is too important not to critically examine the basis. If you disagree, take stock of your own beliefs. Do you give because you believe that a portion belongs the Lord? But it all belongs to the Lord! Do you give because you demand that God give you even more back as a reward? If so, an attitude adjustment is required.

So what is the bottom line—how much should we give? There is no easy answer, but we have an example from the Old Testament: *at least* a tenth. We also have the encouragement of the New Testament: We can't out-give God. As we sow our gifts, God will multiply our resources for further giving. We mustn't give more than we can give with delight, but whatever amount we are led to give, we need to follow through. Which leads me to the idea of giving systematically, or turning our giving intentions into reality.

Chapter 10

Make a Giving Plan

Giving cheerfully, generously, and expectantly are great principles to follow—ones that lead to great joy for others and contentment for ourselves. But I've found that practicing these principles requires careful planning.

On a recent trip to an impoverished region of the former USSR, I frequently encountered destitute men, often missing a limb or their sight, or pathetic old women dressed in rags and begging on the street. After many years of living in Asia, I find my heart curiously indifferent to beggars, yet I want to be sensitive to the Lord's leading to give lovingly to these unfortunates.

Because the neediness in those outstretched hands is so great, sometimes I would become paralyzed by the need and my reluctance to fish around for an appropriate gift, given the circumstances. The solution for me was to determine in advance the largest gift I felt comfortable giving to one of these. I would put that amount in my back left pocket so that as the Lord led, I could immediately retrieve that gift and give it without a great deal of fumbling and groping through my wallet. As a result of my preconceived system, I was able to give regularly and freely to many poor.

While we are to be "Spirit-led" in our giving, that doesn't mean we only give in accordance with sporadic supernatural promptings. A major part of the Spirit-filled life involves the development of habitual ways of behavior that are in keeping with our new nature. This is the root reason for developing spiritual disciplines in all areas of life. It is entirely appropriate, and even necessary, to devise systems that enable us to do what the Spirit directs.

We need to bring the same kind of discipline to our giving that we bring to other areas of Christian living. When the apostle Paul first organized the collection from the Gentile churches to help the poor saints in Jerusalem, he advised the Corinthians, "On the first day of every week, each one of you should set aside a sum of money in keeping with his income, saving it up, so that when I come no collections will have to be made" (1 Corinthians 16:2). While these instructions were made to a specific church in a specific financial situation, they illustrate the principle of systematic giving. "On the first day of every week" implies a regularity that should be a part of our giving, and "in keeping with his income" suggests that what we give should be in proportion to what we earn.

One foundational requirement for giving systematically and proportionately should be obvious: We must keep track of both our income and our giving. I've been surprised, however, to learn how many people don't know how much they make or how much they give. When I was completing my master of divinity degree, I focused my thesis on the attitudes and practices of Campus Crusade staff with regard to giving. I was particularly interested in how their giving practices related to their sense of contentment and prosperity (defined as "living joyfully at the standard of living to which God has called you"). In order to complete my research I surveyed a group of staff on their giving practices. The results of my survey astounded me in several unexpected ways.

For example, every person who participated in my survey indicated that he intended to give away a particular percentage of his income each year. However, not a single respondent could tell me either how much he had earned that year or how much he had given so far that year! In other words, while there was every intention to give a specific amount, there was no mechanism in place to indicate whether or not the goal was being reached. I sadly concluded that most people deluded themselves about their giving, confusing good intentions with reality.

So how can we be more successful in giving faithfully and systematically? First, we need to take stock of our income, then devise a plan that will ensure that we give at the level we set for ourselves in accordance with the Holy Spirit's direction.

It was much simpler to keep track of one's income in Paul's day. Then the laborer usually received his wages on a daily basis. It was a simple matter to count the coins and decide which were to be set aside to be given. Today, thanks to direct deposit and other miracles of modern banking, we seldom even see our paycheck, with the result that it takes more discipline to give regularly and proportionately.

One simple way to get a grip on your income is to take a standard pay period and use it to estimate your annual income. If you get $900 in your paycheck every two weeks, then you are netting

$23,400 annually. You may decide to give 15 percent this year, making your target for giving $3,510. This could be translated into a thermometer chart that could serve as a visual reminder of your intentions throughout the year. By the time December 31 rolled around, you will at least know if you've met your goal!

One practical technique that Kathy and I discovered enables us to accomplish our goals of giving generously as well as systematically. Basically, we enlist the resources of our bank to help us.

We began by opening a second checking account dedicated entirely to giving. This account even paid a small amount of interest, but the main purpose was to separate the money we intended to give from the money we intended to save and spend. Once the account was set up, we arranged for the bank to make an automatic transfer into our giving account each month from our regular checking account. With this one simple move a great deal of stability was brought to our giving. Whenever we wanted to give (either as an ongoing commitment or to meet a special need) we simply wrote a check on our giving account. Everything in that account was, by mutual agreement, dedicated for giving, and we never drew upon it for any other purpose. It was "set aside" in a way comparable with the instructions Paul gave the Corinthians.

One of the factors that makes this system of giving so liberating for us is that, because of our separate giving account, we can arrive at an amount to give that is not constrained by any potential impact on the checkbook out of which we pay our bills and live joyfully. In effect, all of our giving is "pregiven," and all that remains is for us to make the designations and write the checks.

Let me point out, though, that just because we have "pregiven" an amount that corresponds to what we believe God would have us give each pay period, we don't assume that the rest of our resources are untouchable. God could easily impress upon us to give from our day-to-day checkbook as well as from our assets. Remember the key concept: God owns it all!

And that brings us to our conclusion where giving is concerned. We can give during our lifetime, but many forget that we can also give as we leave this world behind. Those who don't have the assurance of eternal life through a personal relationship with Christ often try to avoid thinking about death. Believers, however, should not avoid the wonderful opportunity to bless others and the cause of Christ through final gifts. Wise estate planning is the subject of the next chapter.

Chapter 11

Final Gifts

My ears rang with the badly recorded but greatly amplified wailing of the Muslim call to prayer. (This daily cacophony, plus jet lag, always ensured that I was thoroughly awake at the crack of dawn in a Muslim country.) Later that day I listened open-mouthed as the director of the Campus Crusade for Christ ministry spoke of the amazing openness to the gospel of many in the Middle East. He was telling me how he had allocated his meager budget to allow for giving that would make the largest possible impact, but he had gone out on a limb, ordering ten thousand badly needed copies of *The Story of Jesus* audiotape even though there were no funds for it in his budget.

"Ray, I tell you I prayed and prayed. And then—lo and behold! I receive a telephone call. An American lady has just died, and her will said we are to get money. Just enough money to purchase the tapes I had ordered!"

As I listened, my skin began to tingle. I remembered that Kathy, in her role as the director of planned giving for Campus Crusade, had worked with that same elderly Christian woman a few years before, helping her plan her estate so that when she went to be with the Lord, her assets would continue to work in the harvest field. How amazing that I should be in a position to see with my own eyes the impact of that one woman's posthumous gift!

It's not surprising that people who give generously during their lifetime should want to offer final gifts as they leave this life. The vehicle most people would use to make a final gift is a will, one's last will and testament. I'm convinced that every Christian should have a will and have one at every age. The majority of Christians, however, do not have a will and seem to believe that if they were to die suddenly, then surely others would make reasonable disposition of their assets. What they don't realize is this: If you die with a will, then your wishes determine the disposition of your assets. If you die without a will, the state determines what happens to them.

Even those who do not have significant financial assets may need a will to help determine the disposition of family mementos and heirlooms. Among the items I inherited from my family were a grandfather clock, a painting, and a small book of poetry written by one of my ancestors. These may not have great monetary value, but it is important to me that each item be left to somebody who understands our family history and the significance of these objects. Without a will, the state could distribute these assets, or even order their sale and distribute the proceeds to recipients I wouldn't voluntarily designate.

If you would like to leave something specifically to the work of God's kingdom, then you definitely need to put that in writing. Without a will it is possible that not a cent of your assets will go to that end. With a will, however, you can arrange for your final expenses to be met and leave the balance to further whatever charitable efforts you have found worthy in life.

Making a will needn't be an expensive proposition. While there are books and computer programs that could be used to write one's will, I feel that it is well worth the investment to enlist a competent estate-planning attorney to draft your will professionally. This is especially important for mobile young people, because you will want to be sure your will, even if valid where written, is not rendered invalid because it failed to conform to the law in another state. A will must conform precisely in many technical ways to the local legal requirements, or else it is ignored and the state imposes its own decision on how your assets are to be distributed.

It's entirely possible that a lifetime of giving, saving, and living joyfully on the rest will result in a significant estate—enough money that Uncle Sam could take a chunk of the assets in the form of estate taxes unless you plan ahead to make sure the majority of your assets go where you want them to. One way to minimize tax penalties on the assets you leave behind is to set up a legal entity called a living trust. A living trust is like a bucket. In life we put all of our assets—investment accounts, real estate, etc.—into the bucket. We hold it in life, and in death we pass the bucket and its contents to the trustees specifically named in the trust. The state probate court is not required to assume stewardship of the contents of the bucket, and the assets in the trust never become a matter of public record. Throughout the process there is always a trustee authorized to manage the assets in the bucket, including writing checks immediately after your death.

A trust allows your assets to be transferred quickly to the next generation without the time and expense that it takes for a will to be executed, a process known as probate. While more expensive than a will, a trust greatly eases the transition involved in passing assets from one person to another. A trust can also take advantage of tax-planning strategies that will ensure that Uncle Sam gets the absolute minimum required, which often can be reduced to none at all. This translates, of course, to larger posthumous gifts to your heirs and charitable beneficiaries.

The Bible describes death as the last enemy, but an enemy defeated by the death and resurrection of Christ. Death is not, as New Agers or secularists would have us believe, "just a normal part of life," or merely a transition into another phase of existence. Death is a bad thing, and we feel its evil in every physical failing, ranging from the nagging pain of toothache to the final amnesia of terminal Alzheimer's. Yet the most thrilling aspect of the gospel is that Christ has conquered death and robbed it of its sting. Although each of us will pass through death, its bitterness will be quickly swallowed by the inexpressible joy that follows our entrance into the presence of the Lord. We will take nothing material with us, but through effective estate planning we can be sure that our final gifts continue to enlarge God's kingdom even after we've entered into the presence of the King.

As we've seen, the heart of living joyfully is to relinquish to God what isn't really ours. By practicing the disciplines of giving throughout life, we move into the realm where we can truly live joyfully on the rest. But wait—doesn't God often give us more each day than we actually need? Should we give away every bit of that surplus?

No, I am convinced that God's Word teaches that another portion of our day's income should be set aside to meet future needs. In other words, let's examine what the Bible has to say on the subject of saving.

SECTION 3

SAVING AND
INVESTING BASICS

❖

Planning for an Uncertain Future

Near the end of my years at Duke, I volunteered to drive students to a weekend conference to be held somewhere in the mountains of North Carolina. I say "somewhere," because I had neglected to get directions to the conference site and relied on following another student, who supposedly knew the way.

As the sun set on the hills, I followed his blue, beat-up Volkswagen that was to guide me to our destination. In the growing dusk I tailed him into the mountains and up increasingly remote and winding roads. Finally he pulled off the road and parked at a scenic overlook, where I could see the lights of Raleigh and Durham twinkling in the distance.

Growing impatient after a moment or two, I left my car and stalked up to the VW, now shrouded in darkness. "What in the world are you doing?" I exclaimed in irritation as I put my head inside the driver's window—and interrupted the smooching of a young couple I had never seen in my life. Somehow in the dusk I had begun following the wrong Volkswagen!

I learned a critical lesson in the value of planning. Effective planning would have saved me a great deal of embarrassment and gotten my carload of students to the conference on time.

Most Christians approve of this kind of practical planning, but when it comes to finances, some balk at the common sense and discipline of planning ahead by saving money for future needs. I know some believers who are even theologically opposed to my advice that a portion of what we don't spend should be saved or invested. They consider financial planning somehow unspiritual, claiming that putting aside tangible resources for a "rainy day" denies the principle of faith. The conscientious saver is viewed as putting his faith in his financial assets rather than in the Lord.

Those who condemn saving as failing to trust God have some arguments that sound good at first glance. For example, some point out that, during the forty years of wandering through the Sinai desert, the Israelites were miraculously fed with manna from heaven. Each day they could gather enough manna for that day, but anybody who tried to hoard a two-day supply found that the surplus spoiled immediately. We should be like those Israelites, they say, consuming all of today's provision today and trusting God to provide for tomorrow.

Others who claim that saving is unspiritual point to Jesus' own words:

> Therefore I tell you, do not worry about your life, what you
> will eat or drink; or about your body, what you will wear. Is

not life more important than food, and the body more important than clothes? Look at the birds of the air; they do not sow or reap or store away in barns, and yet your heavenly Father feeds them. Are you not much more valuable than they? Who of you by worrying can add a single hour to his life?

And why do you worry about clothes? See how the lilies of the field grow. They do not labor or spin. Yet I tell you that not even Solomon in all his splendor was dressed like one of these. If that is how God clothes the grass of the field, which is here today and tomorrow is thrown into the fire, will he not much more clothe you, O you of little faith? So do not worry, saying, "What shall we eat?" or "What shall we drink?" or "What shall we wear?" For the pagans run after all these things, and your heavenly Father knows that you need them. But seek first his kingdom and his righteousness, and all these things will be given to you as well. Therefore do not worry about tomorrow, for tomorrow will worry about itself. Each day has enough trouble of its own. (Matthew 6:25-34)

We should be like the flowers and birds, some teach, and make no provision for our personal material needs in the future. Since daisies don't save and sparrows don't have investment accounts, then we shouldn't either. Doesn't saving surplus wealth violate Jesus' instructions?

In order to fully understand Jesus' comments in the passage above, we must consider the context of this teaching about the values and goals we are to have as God's children. In the verses preceding Jesus' admonition, "Therefore I tell you, do not worry...," he explained: "Do not store up for yourselves treasures on earth, where moth and rust destroy, and where thieves break in and steal. But store up for yourselves treasures in heaven, where moth and rust do not destroy, and where thieves do not break in and steal. For where your treasure is, there your heart will be also.... No one can serve two masters. Either he will hate the one and love the other, or he will be devoted to the one and despise the other. You cannot serve both God and Money" (Matthew 6:19-21,24).

The term "money" in this context is not the possession or use of wealth, but refers to the pursuit of wealth for its own sake. It encapsulates the idea of all of the worldly values of the fool who lives as though there is no God. Jesus instructed his listeners to put their ultimate trust in the only true God—the creator of the birds and flowers as well as us—for the provision of their needs. The issue at hand is, "Who are you going to trust? Who are you going to serve?" Jesus commands that we trust in God, not money.

As an inducement to trust God, Jesus points out that while we have no actual control over the future (thieves steal, moths consume, rust corrodes), the One who does control the future cares for us far more than he cares for birds and flowers. Jesus wasn't telling us not to *plan* for the future, but not to *worry* about it.

In fact, I believe that Jesus himself placed a very high value on planning for the future. He prepared for the future, advised his listeners to do the same, and warned of the consequences of not doing so. Even a cursory look at the Gospels reveals that Jesus' whole life was part of a divine master plan. For example, we read in the fourth chapter of John's gospel that on one occasion Jesus surprised his disciples by insisting on traveling through the region of the despised

Samaritans rather than take the customary detour. Jesus' direct path resulted in an entire village acknowledging him as a prophet and even as the Messiah. Had Jesus intended this outcome all along? Was this an example of Jesus' planning for the future? Of course! In fact, Jesus' whole ministry was a carefully unfolding master plan to win our salvation by his death and his resurrection.

In his teaching, Jesus also frequently emphasized planning for the future. He criticized the unbelieving leaders of Israel because they didn't foresee that their rejection of him would lead to their own destruction. In other words, they failed to make plans appropriate to the future that was facing them. Jesus illustrated this principle in the parable of the unjust steward (Luke 16:1-9). This rascal had embezzled his master's money, was about to be fired, and was therefore facing a penniless old age. However, by acting shrewdly (although dishonestly) he used his master's assets to turn his no-win situation into a no-lose situation for himself. Jesus' point was that his enemies should have been as clever and decisive as this sinner. If they had correctly analyzed the precariousness of their situation, they would have planned for the future (one in which Jesus triumphed) rather than be destroyed by their passivity.

The Bible as a whole contains countless illustrations concerning the importance of providing for future contingencies. The patriarch Joseph, for example, was raised up by God to save his family (and the whole population of Egypt for that matter) by prudently storing food during seven years of record harvests to offset the famine that would come during seven years of drought. The book of Proverbs is packed with instructions on the value and practice of the virtue of prudence. Prudence is having the wisdom to foresee a probable course of events and the character to make wise choices in light of that probable future. A prudent individual wears seat belts, for example, not because she expects to be in an accident on a particular trip, but because she foresees the possibility of an accident during any given trip. We don't fault this person for a lack of faith, do we?

When God gives us wealth, it can be seen as a sort of seat belt, a means of protection against the impact of future disasters. Nonbelievers often trust their wealth to insulate them against calamities. Of course, such trust is ultimately misplaced. The Christian who is entrusted with wealth (and we all are) must not trust that wealth but rather the One who gave it. This being understood, if God gives us more than we need for today, logic demands that some of that excess be reserved for tomorrow's needs. This is prudence in action and completely compatible with the teaching of the Bible. It is not a lack of faith to use God's provision to meet life's needs, whether they be today's or tomorrow's.

If we are to put Jesus' teaching on trusting and serving God into practice, then we will need to make some decisions. Choosing to find contentment within our income, rather than on the edge or actually outside of it, means that we will need to make plans to avoid spending it all today (and then some). Just as we are more likely to give generously and regularly if we have an action plan, so are we more likely to make good on our intentions to save if we set some specific goals and take steps to meet them. Let's turn now to some of the basics of saving and investing that will help us prepare to live well in the future.

Everybody Needs
a Cushion

The airport in Kuala Lumpur was dark—even the street sweepers were packing up and going home. I was growing chilly as I sat on a bench outside, guarding my suitcase and hoping even after midnight that someone would miraculously appear waving a sign with my name on it. Alas, I realized that I had been abandoned and was going to be on my own for the night.

I had been told that I would be met and all my expenses would be paid. "Only bring spending money for souvenirs!" Well, I was glad I had disregarded that advice, as I pulled two hundred-dollar bills from the inner recesses of my wallet and was soon on my way to a hotel in a taxi. A flea-bitten flophouse of a hotel, as it turned out, but it was shelter and blessed sleep.

Those hundred-dollar bills were my emergency traveling cushion, and again and again they have saved my bacon as I've traveled around the world for Campus Crusade. As we journey through life, our first financial savings goal should be to accumulate such a cash reserve to cushion us when we encounter the inevitable "emergencies" along the way.

In biblical times, life revolved primarily around agriculture. If crops failed or raiders carried them off, the only safety net was the food that had been put into storage. Today, with our money-based economy, we do the same thing by putting excess income into storage. This cushion serves as a safety net to give us time to restructure our finances in the event of some significant event.

While a couple of hundred-dollar bills served as an adequate cushion when I was stranded at a foreign airport, a bit more than that is required to meet some of the needs that come up for most of us in the course of daily life: major car repairs, unexpected medical bills, emergency airline tickets, etc. If you build up an adequate cash reserve, then if you are injured, you can pay for medical expenses immediately and allow your insurance company to reimburse you later. If you are sued, you can use your cushion to hire a lawyer to defend yourself. If you lose your job, you'll buy some time to find another before your cushion runs out of stuffing.

A good guideline is to have a cushion of sufficient value to cover at least three months of normal living expenses, including housing and car payments, utilities, insurance premiums, and anything else that is a part of your financial reality. The simplest way to calculate this foundational level is to divide your annual income by four. If you earn $28,000 a year, then this cushion would be a fourth of that, or $7,000. A six- to nine-month cushion would be even better, of course, but with even a minimal three-month cushion, you would probably be able to avoid the financial disasters many people face when they've saved nothing for a rainy day.

Without this cushion, any little blip in your income stream could mean a late house payment, an overdue bill, or require you to take out a loan to cover some immediate need. This latter option simply postpones the payment, by the way, but ultimately makes the situation even worse because of the added interest you must repay. Your first savings goal, then, should be to accumulate your cushion so you won't fall into the debt trap with every minor financial emergency.

This is one way people who invest only in their home or retirement funds get into trouble. Even though house payments result in an increase in your ownership-share in a house (often called equity), and even if 401(k) contributions result in a retirement plan with a cash value, this kind of "savings" won't help you much when you're faced with immediate needs. While you can get a loan based on the equity in your home, home-equity loans take time to negotiate and require payback with interest. (In effect, you create two mortgage payments for yourself instead of one.) Sometimes retirement funds can be accessed in an emergency, but even then it is not an overnight process and there are usually significant penalties, including tax consequences, that could destroy a large percentage of the account's value. You can see that neither of these "emergency" sources of funds are truly liquid, and borrowing from them can quickly drain savings you have built up over years.

By the term "liquid" I mean that the money can be accessed easily, with just a phone call or by writing a check. Liquid assets include passbook savings or money-market accounts with check-writing privileges. If an asset takes time to sell or cannot be sold without a significant penalty (such as the early redemption penalty on a certificate of deposit), then the asset is not truly liquid and shouldn't be considered part of your cushion.

There's just no substitute for a three-month cushion, and there's no time like the present for beginning to fund it. I know it's not easy to save for a rainy day when present wants and needs are clamoring for your hard-earned dollars. But even saving a tiny proportion of whatever income you earn will help establish this critical discipline and make you feel more prepared for unforeseen financial needs.

What if, while saving to complete your cushion, you experience some financial emergency, such as a major car repair? Try to keep saving, even if you have to cut back the amount to a dribble. Do whatever is in your power (short of borrowing) to avoid interrupting the funding of your emergency reserve. Even if you have to dip into your half-made cushion to deal with the immediate emergency, then try to double the rate at which you fund the cushion until you are back on schedule. Eat rice and beans, if necessary, but fund that cushion!

This will result in several positive outcomes. You will complete the funding of the cushion, and that task will move from the realm of wishful thinking into the realm of reality. It will also discipline you for the ongoing task of living within your income while continuing to save for more long-range needs. Again, I realize you may be facing a common dilemma: low income, high cost of living, myriad demands on what little you have. But the best way to build a different future is to begin saving today, even when it seems impossible. You might be surprised to discover how much you can save each month simply by emptying your pockets or purse of change every day and making that pile of coins the first thin layer of your cushion.

Once you've funded your prudent cash reserve over time, you'll be free to invest future surplus in savings plans that have more potential to "work" for you—that is, give you a greater return on your investment. Let me introduce the concept of the investment pyramid, a savings strategy you'll want to build into your overall financial plan.

Imagine a pyramid with four distinct levels. Each level must be constructed on top of the one before it, and no step can be skipped. Each higher level is built on a larger foundational level. Built in this way, a pyramid is a strong and stable structure. Constructed upside down, or with missing layers, the structure is far from ideal and potentially disastrous.

Think of the bottom layer of the pyramid as your cushion—a liquid reserve significant enough to be drawn upon when immediate needs arise. The next level of the investment pyramid contains conservative investment vehicles that provide a healthy long-term return on your contributions. The third level of the pyramid is made up of more aggressive investments that offer the possibility of higher returns, but also carry more risk of loss. The top level (the smallest point of the pyramid) should consist of the most speculative investments—those that have great earnings potential but also great risk.

My point is, once your cushion is funded, don't stop saving! Rather, begin to redirect your savings stream into the next (second) level of the investment pyramid. (I'll explain how to fund the rest of your pyramid in the next chapter.) Saving shouldn't be a short-term event, but a long-term commitment. Meanwhile, try to keep a couple of hundred-dollar bills tucked away in your wallet in case you're ever stranded far away from home!

Chapter 14

Investing for the Long Haul

My kids loved water pistols, and I still do, having found that one serves wonderfully to remind our cat, Stormy, that it's *not* okay to demand that we feed him just because the sun happens to be up. Investing is kind of like playing with a water pistol, or perhaps a garden hose, filling first one bucket and then another.

You'll be glad to know that the basic bucket-filling skills you develop while completing a solid foundation (cash cushion) for your pyramid will be used again and again as you continue to build the upper three levels. You never turn the hose (saving stream) off, but you move on to a new target once a given bucket is full.

I believe that building a stable investment pyramid is simply good stewardship in action. In Matthew 25, the disciple recounted Jesus' parable of the talents in which each of three stewards was entrusted with a certain amount of wealth. The ones Jesus commended were those who recognized God's ownership of what had been given to them and who invested those assets wisely. The only one Jesus criticized was the steward who hid the wealth entrusted to him rather than shrewdly putting those assets to work for his master. Conclusion? Put God's money to work!

Once the bottom level of your pyramid is stable, it's time to start funding the second level, consisting of conservative investments that will give you a long-term return on your investment. This part of your pyramid, consisting of carefully chosen investment vehicles such as growth-oriented mutual funds, will provide the means for you to buy a home, fund your children's education, or meet your needs in retirement. Ideally, all three goals will be met!

Even those who complete the foundational level of their financial pyramid often neglect the second level. They reason that the equity in their house, their company retirement program, or their parents' wealth that they may someday inherit makes it unnecessary to fund this level of the pyramid. Besides, that percentage of their income can be well spent now on lots of other things. *Carpe diem*—let's live for today!

But none of us knows the future. Our parents could spend "our" inheritance—which they have every right to do, by the way. Our company could go bankrupt, taking our pension with it (although this is very unlikely considering the strict laws that protect pension funds). The real estate market could collapse, as it did in California in the early 1990s, and our home equity could become a negative number! The purpose of the conservative investment level of your pyramid is to cushion you against the consequences of such large economic events as well as to provide prudently for those you love and your own needs in the future.

Since a major goal of investing beyond the cash-cushion stage involves planning for a time when we will no longer have our usual monthly income (retirement), it's wonderful that our government has provided tax-sheltered opportunities to save toward that goal. One common tax-sheltered investing plan is called an IRA, or individual retirement account. Another similar plan is called a 401(k) and does the same thing: You sock away contributions without having to pay taxes until you take out the money during retirement. In theory, you are liable for more taxes during your earning years, so it should prove quite a benefit to pay lower postretirement taxes on money earned while you were younger.

If you have any opportunities to participate in a company-sponsored retirement plan—401(k), 403(b), or similar—be sure to do so, especially if your employer matches a portion of your contribution. That's free money! However, since that money can only be drawn upon at retirement (usually at age sixty-five), make sure that it's not the only egg in your investment basket. You should never loot your IRA to buy a house, for example, or help your kids with college expenses.

So what kinds of investments are appropriate for this second—or conservative—level of your investment pyramid? Beginners in investing encounter an incredible array of jargon, acronyms, and other insider terms. Jumping into the world of Wall Street can be intimidating for those of us who were raised on piggy banks and passbook savings accounts. Unless you are motivated by God to invest his resources wisely, you probably won't persist long enough to understand what modern investments are all about. But you absolutely can (and must) learn enough so that your participation in the financial market goes beyond blind chance and dumb luck!

For starters, forget everything you've ever heard about "playing the market," implying that Wall Street is nothing more than Las Vegas on the Hudson. Modern investment vehicles are really nothing more than a way to entrust your money to others who are busy earning money and could use yours to earn a bit more. When you buy shares in a company—its stock—you are buying a tiny chunk of the whole and giving the company some of your money with which to do business.

If you invest in Intel, for example, your dollars may be used to research new chip designs, build advanced processing plants, or fund marketing campaigns designed to sell more Intel products. Ideally, the end result of your investment is that Intel makes more money, and shares in a profitable company are more valuable than a less-profitable company. Result: Intel succeeds, and you succeed with it.

The modern economy offers countless ways to put money to work in the financial infrastructure on which modern wealth is built. Jesus lived in a time long before the modern stock market, but there is no doubt that he was familiar with all of the concepts involved. Consider again his parable of the talents. The master in the story followed several basic investment principles that still make sense today.

First, he diversified. He didn't put all his assets in the hands of a single individual. Of course, had he done so he would have had an excellent return had he chosen the first two stewards as his financial managers. But he would have risked losing it all if he had given it to the one described as wicked, lazy, and worthless.

We need to be sure that we diversify as well. If we pick what we believe to be three excellent companies and invest in the stock of each one, it is very likely that one will outperform the average of the three and one will do less well than the others. Instead of worrying about the poorer performers, we look at the aggregate performance of the whole. This principle of diversification is a critical aspect of making wise investments. Even if you invest only in companies you believe are well-run industry leaders and market a great product, you could lose money! Spreading your investments among a mix of stocks, mutual funds, and bonds minimizes the chance that all will fall in value simultaneously.

Another principle followed by the investor in Jesus' parable is this: Dump your losers and switch what remains to winners. The investor kept tabs on his investments, and even though the lazy steward would doubtless have preferred to be left alone with his loot indefinitely, the master demanded an accounting. We should learn from his resulting action: He took what remained (fortunately, all of his principal) and put it in the hands of those who had so skillfully doubled his assets.

At the risk of squeezing the parable for more than Jesus meant it to say, let me point out that the investor in the parable also made moral judgments about those with whom he entrusted his assets. I think we should do the same. For example, recently there has been a lot of interest in tobacco stocks, and distilling industries are periodically rated as good investments. Thinking cynically, I suppose it will always be good business to sell cigarettes and booze. But would Jesus want us to put his money into service pandering to the vices of our neighbors? I hardly think so. We should be aware of the ways and means that various companies use our money in their business.

How can we put all the principles Jesus illustrated into shoe leather in today's investment marketplace? It is difficult to find a better choice of investments than several quality mutual funds chosen strategically for their potential for long-term growth. A mutual fund is like an investment club: All of the members pool their assets and proceed to buy a widely diversified mix of stocks, bonds, and other investment vehicles. The whole group, then, shares in the profits of the combined pool of investments. The wonderful thing about a mutual fund is that your ownership in one represents a small share of a very large basket full of expertly (we hope) selected eggs. If a few of those eggs turn out to be cracked, your losses are offset by the larger number of winners.

Mutual funds are run by professional managers, many of whom are rewarded financially to the extent that their funds perform well. They have a lot of motivation to invest your assets wisely and are much more likely to pick well-performing assortments of investments than most of us could do on our own. Resist the temptation to fund the second level of your pyramid with a handful of individual stocks. Instead use resources such as *Money* magazine's annual report or the quarterly summaries in the *Wall Street Journal* on the best-performing mutual funds to select three or four in which to invest.

Sometimes your company-sponsored tax-sheltered savings plans will only offer a narrow range of investment options. What should you do then? If those options perform as well as the top-tier mutual funds listed in the sources mentioned above, then great! If they don't, talk to your company's representative for pensions and retirement accounts. It may be possible to add highly regarded mutual funds to the company's program or to gain the option of taking complete direction of your tax-sheltered retirement accounts. As a last resort, it may be possible to remove your IRA assets into a self-directed investment program with a top-rated mutual fund company.

I indicated that completing your three-month cushion was the signal to begin funding the second level (conservative) of the investment pyramid, but I don't know of any obvious way to trigger the funding of the third level, consisting of aggressive investments. Perhaps if the value of your conservative level is on the order of a year's salary you could consider diverting your savings stream into the third level of the investment pyramid.

You may be wondering exactly how to define "conservative," "aggressive," and "speculative." While there are no exact definitions, obviously the terms imply a series of steps from safe, stable assets (mutual funds jammed with high-quality "blue chip" stocks) to some more risky investments with greater potential for growth. Investments in the third (aggressive) level could include mutual funds that are more assertively managed than those more appropriate for the conservative level. Funds in the third level might be heavily weighted with technology stocks, for example. This level might also include individual stocks that are selected for their growth potential, but most people would find it safer and wiser to select mutual funds that have aggressive growth as their management objective.

Another key factor to consider when funding the second and third levels of your pyramid is the number of years until you plan to retire and how large your nest egg has already grown. If you're young, you can afford a more aggressive mix of investments in the lower levels of your pyramid. If you won't need to live off the money you invest for another thirty years or so, you can afford to take some hits, even losing much of your principal, and still be able to start over in time to make up the difference by the time you retire. If you're already nearing retirement age, however, you would not want to put a significant portion of your investment portfolio at risk. In this case, you should pursue a safe-and-sane investment policy and earmark only a small percentage of your assets for highly aggressive (i.e., volatile) investment vehicles.

As the years go by and your investment pyramid becomes more fully formed by consistent building, you will eventually be ready to fund the topmost level, comprising the very peak of the pyramid. This level should consist of the most speculative investments, including more volatile stocks or mutual funds, real estate (either actual properties or shares in funds that invest in real estate), assets that you expect to rise dramatically in price (rare coins, fine art, etc.), or even options (financial "bets" that a given stock or commodity will rise or fall in price). The reason this speculative level should contain only a small proportion of your total assets is obvious: These long shots often don't pay off. You should never fund this level until the lower three are reasonably solid.

If your eyes are starting to glaze over because you're not familiar with basic investment concepts and terminology, please don't become intimidated. I am convinced that ordinary individuals can learn the basics of investment and may not need to rely heavily on professional financial advisers. However, if a financial planner can provide you with the necessary initial motivation to put your financial house in order or give you sound and objective advice when you're in a complicated situation, then by all means, find a trustworthy one.

My own preference would be an adviser who is a certified financial planner (CFP) rather than a broker who makes his living by selling investments. I would want a professional adviser who was dedicated to educating and motivating me rather than trying to sell me something. I recommend seeking out someone who, for a fixed fee, will analyze your financial situation and recommend a specific investment strategy that makes sense for you based on your age, assets, personal risk tolerance, and short- and long-term goals. Having a strategy you understand and can execute puts you in charge of your financial objectives. As you age and change some of your goals over time, your investment strategy will also change. A good financial planner will help you customize your strategy as your objectives change.

I hope you'll walk away from this chapter with one key objective in mind: to faithfully manage the surplus wealth God has put into your hands. Personally, I don't ever want to face Jesus and hear him say, "Where are the results of all the wealth with which I blessed you? Don't tell me you consumed ALL of it!" On the contrary, at the end of my life I want to be able to look my Master in the eye and hear him say, "Well done, good and faithful servant! You have been faithful with relatively unimportant wealth; now prepare to receive true riches!"

Chapter 15

Start Now!

Even when we understand the basics of saving and investing wisely, following through will still require discipline. It is so tempting to say to ourselves, "I'll begin saving next month—I really need every bit of my income right now to get over this hump." Believe me, that "hump" will never go away! No matter what your current situation is, you will probably never find it any easier to adopt the discipline of saving than right now.

If you're still not as motivated as you'd like to be, let me entice you with another financial principle: The near-magical ingredient in causing money to multiply is not so much how *much* you save, but how *long* you allow your money the luxury of compounding. Compounding is the process by which money, when invested, multiplies itself, and is another crucial reason to start early, even when you have only a little.

As a fresh-faced lieutenant in the air force I was frequently the target of subtle jokes played oh so discreetly by the enlisted personnel I supervised—such as finding an index card on my desk with the words, "How to amuse a lieutenant for hours—see other side." As you might guess, the other side had the same message.

I was completely taken in by another favorite joke—a quarter stuck to the floor with epoxy glue. My face reddened thoroughly as a group of NCOs guffawed at my hapless scrabbling at the immovable coin. I joined the laughter as gracefully as I could, but it dawned on me that the tricksters obviously thought that anyone who would stoop to pick up anything less than folding money was absurdly tight-fisted, as though time were too precious to stoop to retrieve a single errant coin. I, however, had come to realize the value of even a single cent!

Benjamin Franklin is credited with the proverb, "A penny saved is a penny earned," but a version that takes into account the value of money over time might be, "A penny saved is worth $137.81 in only a hundred years!" Many people don't understand the significance of the way money increases its value over time. Everyone who has ever had a passbook savings account as a child knows that $10.00 saved for a year at an interest rate of 3 percent earns an additional thirty cents in interest. Big deal! But the miracle of compounding becomes evident when that $10.30 earns thirty-one cents, and that $10.61 earns thirty-two cents, and so on. The growth is slow at first, but ultimately rockets to unbelievable heights.

When my daughter, Laurie, was in high school, she once spent some time with a young man named Jerry. One day I asked him, "Tell me, Jerry—do you think a janitor could ever become a millionaire?" He allowed that it was quite possible—if the janitor bought a winning lottery ticket! I suggested that he could become

a millionaire purely as a result of saving a tenth of his income—
even if he didn't get a single raise during his career.

Jerry and I plugged some numbers into a financial calculator
program on my computer that assumed that the janitor earned
$25,000 annually. We agreed that he saved a tenth of it at a rate
matching the average return of the New York Stock Exchange for
the past fifty years, about 12 percent. Finally, we even stipulated
that the janitor would retire early, at the age of sixty instead of the
more standard sixty-five. When the program calculated the value
of the janitor's savings at retirement—not counting other pensions
or Social Security—Jerry was staggered by the result: $1,106,481.84!

"Why, I could be a millionaire!" he exclaimed. I agreed, silently
wondering if I had chosen too apt a profession for my example.
After all, this guy was dating my daughter. I set that thought aside
and pointed out that if he also participated in a company-sponsored
retirement plan and took Social Security benefits into account, he
would be worth much more than a million dollars.

We continued our discussion, except that I introduced a second janitor employed on the same basis as the first. There was one
difference: This janitor reasoned that he was young, so why not live
a little? There was plenty of time to save later. So this janitor spent
the tenth that the other saved, generally living right up to the edge
of his income. To his credit, he never went into debt, but after
twenty years of declining to save he realized that he was now forty
and had only twenty more years to work before retiring with his
fellow janitor.

Now the second janitor became really serious about saving, but,
like his pal, he hadn't received a raise in all those years and wouldn't

get one either. So what would he have to put away each year to catch up with the first janitor?

We plugged in some numbers. What if he saved 20 percent of his income? To Jerry's surprise, his savings over the next twenty years would grow to a relatively pathetic $286,375. What if he saved a whopping 50 percent of his income? Even at this draconian rate, his account at retirement would only contain $715,938. We raised the savings rate higher and higher. Finally, at the impossible savings rate of 70 percent of his annual income, the second janitor finally came to the point where his net worth at retirement would just pass the million dollar mark. To actually surpass the first janitor, the second would have to save at a rate greater than 77 percent for his final two decades on the job!

Jerry was impressed by this comparison. Obviously, saving 10 percent is possible, while saving 77 percent of a modest fixed income is not. The difference between these two numbers highlights one of the subtlest (and most wonderful) aspects of investing: The first dollars you save are worth a great deal more than dollars saved later in life. And this happens because of the principle of compounding! Of course, my example ignored other factors, such as inflation, but it also omitted the possibility of a raise or switching to a more lucrative line of work.

The action point is simple: Start saving now. Most people reason the way the second janitor did. They think, "We have plenty of time to save later. There are so many expenses now, and we make so little. Saving now just isn't feasible." What this reasoning overlooks is that even though income may increase in the future (of course, it may not), the value of money saved early quickly surpasses the value of money saved later. Using the same financial assumptions as I did in the story of the janitors, a single dollar saved forty years ago is today worth $45. A single dollar saved twenty years ago is worth less than $7. That same dollar saved for only ten years wouldn't even buy a Happy Meal at McDonald's!

If you're saying to yourself, "My situation is exactly like that of the second janitor!" are you financially doomed? Not in a universe in which God is ultimately in control. While it's important to start saving early, it's never too late to start. After all, my example of the janitor millionaires may have created the wrong impression. We don't need to be millionaires; we need to be faithful stewards of God's assets. Even if we're starting quite late to manage our money wisely, it's a case of better late than never. And just as God multiplied the food of an aged and penniless widow (see 1 Kings 17:7-16), God can supply our needs in old age.

When Kathy and I joined the staff of Campus Crusade for Christ we realized that the relatively fixed nature of our salary meant that we could not expect much greater income in the future. That observation motivated us to save aggressively in our earliest years. We made many sacrifices, convinced that it was only prudent to make provision for an uncertain future. While the going was sometimes tough, we were motivated to stay on our course as we observed the careers of our contemporaries. Many of our peers in the business world were taking starter jobs in enterprises with great potential for advancement. They felt they could afford to start saving later, but most never did because of an important psychological factor: There is no easy time to begin the process of saving a portion of one's income. Expenses chase income so closely that unless one develops the grit and discipline to save on a small income, he or she will most assuredly find it just as difficult to start saving later.

The moral should be obvious: It's never too early or too late (and you're never really too poor) to start saving, even if it's only 3 percent of your income. Start now, even if money is scarce and it takes discipline to save. Your discipline will reap several harvests—in your character, in your financial life, and in bringing honor to God for living within your income both now and in the future. Remember: It never gets easier to start saving! But the rewards are sure.

Chapter 16

Hold On and Enjoy the Ride

One festive night in Mexico City, while enjoying dinner with a group of colleagues who were assisting me in teaching an extension course, I happened to hear a few snatches in Spanish from the television over the bar. I didn't have to be a Berlitz scholar to recognize that something big was happening. It turned out to be that the financial markets in New York had plunged almost five hundred points in a single day! Black Monday was how that day came to be known, and it was a great reminder that what God has given, God can take away.

If you're diligent in building your investment pyramid, a time may come when you see the value of your investments shrink noticeably over a period of months, or even in a single day. The ups and downs of the financial market are indeed like a roller coaster sometimes, and you'll need a strong stomach and a good grip if you're going to ride. Most important, you'll need to keep your faith firmly rooted in the Ruler of the universe rather than in the world economy.

As I'm writing, the financial markets in America have seen an unprecedented rise in the value of many stocks. Some, especially the so-called Internet stocks, have risen in such a way as to give new meaning to the word *meteoric*. This causes even the most steady-minded investor to have qualms. If one has seen the value of his or her investments increase dramatically, there is a nagging sense of unease that they could plummet just as quickly. On the other hand, if one's investments have stayed in the doldrums, or even dropped, one may feel chagrin for having missed one of the great investment opportunities of the century.

Of course, by the time these words are read, the world's entire financial picture might have changed dramatically. Which brings me to my point: The market goes both up and down. That's just the way it is, and wishing it had gone higher or wouldn't go lower is like wishing fish weren't slimy.

For those of us who believe in the sovereignty of God, great comfort comes from remembering that whatever financial gains we enjoy or losses we suffer are ultimately in his hands. After all, it isn't our money, right? As stewards of God's resources, we are responsible for faithfully using the assets he has lent us to the best of our ability. We are not responsible for whether our investments perform spectacularly or dismally in response to economic forces over which we have no control.

When we experience the inevitable ups and downs of the financial market, it's tempting to become either cocky or fearful. In the first case, if the assets under our management grow meteorically, there is a temptation to regard them more as "ours" and less as "God's." It becomes easy to choose a higher and higher standard of living, rather than prayerfully and deliberately choosing to live at whatever standard to which God has called us. It grows deceptively easy to make large expenditures without serious investigation into whether this is what our Master would wish us to do with this windfall. Increasing assets also tempt us to trust in material wealth and do little to encourage us to live in humble dependence on God, as we would if we really needed him to provide our "daily bread."

In the second case, when assets suddenly shrink as a result of certain economic forces, the temptation is to allow a little worm of fear to begin gnawing at our faith. "If the market crashes, what will happen to me?" If we allow it to do so, that little worm will begin to eat the joy right out of our Christian life. "What will I eat? What will I wear?" These were some of the hypothetical questions Jesus dealt with in his Sermon on the Mount when he pointed out that since God feeds the birds, surely he will feed us too.

If you're a believer, then you don't have to be emotionally and spiritually rocketed high and low by the upswings and downturns of the market. The Lord is still your shepherd. You need not fear crashes, depressions, recessions, the Fed clamping down on interest rates, the triple witching hour, or any of the other financial bogeymen that haunt the nightmares of investors who have assumed personal ownership of the Lord's assets. In fact, Kathy and I have used financial reversals to remind us of the essentials of being faithful stewards of God's assets. Have we been giving generously? Have we been consuming beyond the standard of living to which God has called us?

That being said, there are other practical attitudes and behaviors that we need to practice during market fluctuations. The first and possibly most crucial attitude is to remember that you're investing for the long haul, not the one-hundred-yard dash. What markets do on a month-to-month basis isn't nearly as important as what they do from decade to decade. There's not a single ten-year period in this century during which common stocks did not outperform every other investment vehicle, and that includes the huge market drop that took place in 1929, which paved the way for the Great Depression. While past performance does not guarantee future results, it indicates that stocks will probably continue to be the wisest investment choice for many years to come. The wise investor knows that the stocks he buys today may be worth less tomorrow, but in a decade those same stocks are likely to be worth more than any other reasonable investment.

In general, then, our response to a severe pounding when the market drops should be to sit tight or even to buy more high-quality investments while they may be significantly undervalued. Resist the temptation to sell off your investments in a falling market! If you bought for the long term (five years or more), then it is very likely that your investments will recover and grow.

Even if the market undergoes a significant correction, taking some of "our" assets down with it, we will do well to remember the words of the Psalmist: "This is the day the LORD has made; let us rejoice and be glad in it" (Psalm 118:24). On that day, like any other, God holds our lives in his hands and counts us very precious. When the financial market has a hiccup or even a full-fledged choking fit, we still remember that our life is God's and our assets are his. If he should choose to take them all, we'll still trust him. But until that happens, we'll enjoy the ride!

Now that we've covered the stewardship basics of "give some" and "save some," we come to the part of personal financial management where most people believe that they are specially gifted: spending it! Yes, from now on we'll concentrate on the last piece of Johnny Boswell's good advice: *live joyfully on the rest.*

SECTION 4

———

LIVING JOYFULLY
ON THE REST

❖

Chapter 17

The Fallacy of Easy Credit

The story of the dueling janitors in chapter 15 should give you hope! Even when your income is small, time usually makes even a little grow into quite a lot. There is another moral to the story, however—one not so obvious. The story shows how money multiplies itself over time when invested. The opposite happens when money is borrowed. To put it another way, debt grows at a similar rate, except debt is more like a cancer eating at your financial organs.

Let's suppose that you and your best friend are going to buy neighboring houses of exactly the same value for a selling price of $100,000. Let's assume that you have saved $10,000 to put into your house purchase as a down payment. You get a loan for $90,000 on a fixed-rate mortgage of 9 percent that runs forty years to maturity. This is the longest standard mortgage period, but leads to a lower monthly payment than a more traditional thirty-year loan.

Your best friend can get the same terms (9 percent interest for forty years) on a no-money-down loan of $100,000.

So what good has it done you to save that $10,000? Both you and your friend are going to wind up owning identical houses in forty years, right? The only difference is that your friend will pay a little more each month because he or she has borrowed $10,000 more than you have. It might appear that you should have enjoyed spending the $10,000 like your friend did. But consider this question: How much does it actually cost your friend to borrow that final $10,000, which you had previously saved?

His payment for the nothing-down option is $804.62, while your payment for the $10,000-down option is $724.16. This may not seem like much of a difference, but let's see what this difference is over a forty-year period. We can do this by pretending that we are investing the difference ($80.46) under the same terms that the first janitor saved his nest egg. The value of that difference after forty years—when each house is fully paid off—is $427,332. In other words, if you made the deal with the $10,000 down payment and simply invested the difference between your house payment and your friend's over those four decades, you would wind up with $427,332 to show for it plus a paid-off house! Your friend, because of his failure to put $10,000 into the house, paid enough extra to the mortgage company so that they, not he, made almost half a million dollars more on his loan.

Imagine that the two of you were meeting with the same loan officer when setting up your house purchases. The officer tells you, "With your deal you get the title to the house at the end of the term of the loan and, oh yes, also this check for $427,332 from your investment brokers. Your friend, however, gets only the title to the house."

"What!?" shrieks your friend. "For the lack of a lousy $10,000 down payment I'm to be penalized almost HALF A MILLION DOLLARS?!"

That's the way it works—money invested grows over time, and money borrowed makes money for the lender, not you. If you were to compare the value of money saved versus the value of money borrowed, I guarantee that you would never hear the words "no money down" the same way again!

If more people knew this, they would save more and would begin saving earlier in their lives. They would also borrow less, right? Actually, I'm not sure they would. So many of us simply have not developed the discipline to save for future needs, and borrowing in order to get both basics and luxuries has become deeply embedded in our culture. Even if we have saved, sometimes unexpected emergencies wipe out our funds and then we have a hard time getting back into the saving cycle—and choosing a lower standard of living while we do.

I don't mean to give the impression that I am completely "anti-debt." I think there are some circumstances in which debt is appropriate, such as when taking out a mortgage on a house. (We'll talk more about this in chapter 25.) I see debt as being very much like fire: a great blessing when under our control, and a great threat when raging without restraint. The Bible has a lot to say about the evils of indebtedness, but to be fair it also commends those who are willing to lend to alleviate suffering (see Psalm 112:5, for example). But just as we teach children to fear fire before we teach them how to kindle it, I would like to analyze some of the dangers of debt before looking at the blessings that can result from money borrowed wisely.

Debt has become a source of deep oppression to the average American. The typical worker is indebted not only for a house and car (or cars), but also may be carrying a large school loan and one or more overdue credit card accounts, each of which is accruing interest for the lender at a furious rate. Why are so many of us in this predicament? Debt is just so easy to acquire!

Our whole culture is based on the idea popularized by the McDonald's mantra: "You deserve a break today!" The key words are "deserve" and "today." The first word carries with it the oft-heard assurance that whatever you want, you should have. Instant gratification is the bedrock of the philosophy of consumerism, a philosophy that encourages people to have more, use more, and spend more, preferably without limit and without delay. Few of those messages the media slings at us say, "Delay gratification! Put off fulfillment! You'll appreciate it more if you earn it yourself!"

I realize, of course, that McDonald's is only trying to sell another couple of billion hamburgers and didn't craft its advertising campaign for the purpose of indoctrinating us into the evils of consumerism. Still, the company's slogan reflects the prevailing world-view, especially its emphasis on "I want it now!" You don't deserve a break later or tomorrow or when you've earned one, says the jingle. You deserve a break *today*. Don't put off your well-deserved (not necessarily well-earned) break for another microsecond!

What does all of this have to do with debt? Simply this: The full force of our culture is telling us to "Just Do It!"—and the mechanism for doing it now is acquiring debt. We are not only being sold products, but the debt that makes it possible to buy the products. Just keep your eyes open for a day or two and note the number of times you are offered credit. You will be amazed.

Obviously, I recommend avoiding most debt like the plague. However, when people are beginning to make better financial choices, they often find themselves saddled with a load of debt they've spent years accumulating. So how should they deal with that existing obligation?

If you find yourself in this quandary and your debt is long term and at a relatively low interest rate (such as a school loan), and you do not yet have that three-month cushion of liquid assets, I would suggest that you build that cushion from the amount you set aside for saving and make your debt payments out of the rest you intend to live on. It will be tough, but it's important to keep on saving (or begin saving) as well as to pay off debt. Don't let yourself become comfortable with debt. Instead, train yourself to see debt as the enemy, as a hostile raider intent on robbing you of the pleasure of living joyfully on what God gives you.

In the next chapter we'll talk more about what you should do if you've already succumbed to the seduction of easy credit and are tired of the slavery that the debt-oppressed eventually feel. If your debt is in the form of short-term high-interest credit card debt, then it's time to pull out all the stops. Few things will steal the joy of living on what God has provided more than being chased by Credit Card Monster.

Chapter 18

Slaying the Credit Card Monster

Of all the debt merchants, the credit card hucksters are probably the most aggressive. Each week I receive offers to apply for new credit cards and am assured that my application would be accepted with delight. It ought to be—the interest I would have to pay on an overdue credit card account could be greater than 25 percent per year! What creditor wouldn't be delighted with that kind of return on an investment?

One of the dangers of credit card debt is that you just don't see it coming. Sure, you've racked up a few thousand dollars (hasn't everyone?), but paying the minimum each month isn't that much of a budgetary strain. Then suddenly a visit to the emergency room or a blown transmission or an encounter with an uninsured motorist, and a second card has a few thousand dollars on it. By this time you're a hooked fish and don't even know that you're only a few moments from being gutted and cooked over the roasting coals of some credit company.

Here's a miniquiz to see if you're already on your way to the barbecue.

Do you...

- occasionally skip payments on credit cards?

- pay only the monthly minimum the credit card company requires?

- consolidate credit card balances by opening new accounts and transferring balances?

If you've answered yes to any of these, you could already be in trouble. How much trouble? Well, national credit card statistics indicate that the average American consumer with a credit card debt of $5,000 (at a 20 percent annual interest rate) will take over five years to repay that debt. Five years of financial slavery, when negligible savings are being accumulated—and all for a debt no bigger than a used car! It's easy to see how with larger debts, for example, $20,000, one could easily reach a place where simply paying the minimum each month could consume 20 to 30 percent of one's income.

I suggested previously that with moderate amounts of debt at modest interest rates it is possible to combine debt-reduction with savings, especially when you're just beginning to fund your three-month cushion. However, if you have several maxed-out credit cards and thousands of dollars of high-interest debt, don't wait another minute to start cornering the Credit Card Monster.

First, aggressively seek a card with a lower interest rate and transfer your whole debt to the new lower rate. Then seek to put every available cent—as much as 25 percent of your total income—into reducing that debt. Make paying that debt your top financial priority.

Second, get professional help. Seek out a financial counseling service that will help you get control of your debt. There are several Christian ministries, easily accessible via the Internet, that can help greatly (for example, http://www.turningpoint.org). What these organizations will typically do for little or no cost is help you analyze your income and debt to ascertain how much per month can be directed toward debt elimination. They will collect all your credit cards and negotiate with all your creditors for reduced interest rates. Finally, they will consolidate all of your payments into a single payment for the duration of the debt elimination period. (Note: This should never involve a debt consolidation loan. Why borrow more money at a high interest rate when this is what caused the problem in the first place?)

While an extremely motivated individual can do these things without outside help, there are good reasons for using a good debt-management organization. They already have the systems in place to do easily what might be difficult for you as an individual, such as negotiate with credit card companies for reduced (or even zero) interest rates. They can easily take your one monthly payment and pay off all your accounts with minimum paperwork and no chance of overlooking one or more creditors. If your income should increase, you can let them know and they will help recalculate a new monthly payback amount to reduce your debts to zero even faster.

Yes, Virginia, there really are agencies and ministries out there that will help people in all these ways! Some are supported by donations and are a ministry to the community at large, while others are funded by creditors who would rather be paid than see the poor consumer driven to bankruptcy.

Do I have to mention that bankruptcy should be avoided? Even though it often appears to be the easy way out, I believe God would have us be responsible by repaying our just debts. A believer in my church saw his business imitate the *Titanic,* leaving him stuck with close to a million dollars of debt. Even well-meaning Christians urged him to declare bankruptcy, but he trusted God to help him repay every cent, and he did.

Many people in trouble with credit card debt fear the consequent impact on their credit rating. In my not-so-humble opinion, concern over one's creditworthiness is a grave symptom of a deeper problem. Why not focus instead on how to live on what God provides rather than scheme to borrow more of what God hasn't yet given (and might never give)? If a credit card disaster totally ruins your credit rating so that for the rest of your life you have to live on a cash basis, it could turn out to be a great financial blessing. This alone could force you to save for major purchases, enabling you to avoid interest payments as well as earn interest or dividends while accumulating assets. And in reality, a person who assumes control of an otherwise unmanageable credit card problem has already taken the first steps toward credit rehabilitation. After a few years of responsible payments, a host of easy credit offers will once again be flooding your mailbox!

If you are only starting down the slippery slope of accumulating credit card debt, it's not too late to take less extreme measures. First, destroy all your cards except perhaps for one. Take that single card, seal it inside a Ziploc bag, then bury it in the deepest recesses of your freezer. Next, decide if you can live on 65 percent of your income, and earmark the rest for giving and debt-elimination. If you can't live on 65 percent, try 70 or 75 percent, but live on the bare minimum.

Prayerfully decide what percentage you would like to give (your giving should continue no matter what), and give it promptly each pay period. Then take the rest of the earmarked funds and use them to make all of your minimum payments, putting the balance into paying off the credit card with the smallest amount outstanding. When that card is paid off, keep pouring the whole percentage into paying minimums on each card, with the rest going toward the card with the next smallest balance, etc., until all your credit cards are paid off. And then—celebrate! Readjust your percentages into more appropriate investing and giving streams. At last you will have slain the Credit Card Monster. Of course, far better that you never have to face him in the first place!

My bottom-line advice is: Be eager to repay debt and reluctant to incur it. If you are committed to living joyfully on what you earn, you will pray long and hard before incurring debt for any reason. And when you have debt, you will seek to pay it back as soon as possible.

Remember, we are children of the King, born to serve him freely with all that we are and have. Don't voluntarily mortgage your future (and your children's) by needlessly incurring debt. Declare your commitment to be independent from debt today. Fighting the debt monster is no fun.

Chapter 19

Bending Credit Cards
to Your Will

Every little boy loves things that go BOOM! As a preteen consumer of comic books, I would scrutinize the ads that appeared in the back of *Superman, Sergeant Rock,* and *Turok, Son of Stone* comics. Did those x-ray glasses really work? Could I learn to easily hypnotize others and bend them to my will? I was fascinated by the picture of a miniature cannon that fired thousands of explosive reports using only a few cents worth of a "perfectly safe" but unnamed fuel.

Just as the idea of a "perfectly safe" explosive substance seems unlikely yet intriguing, so is the idea of bending the power of credit cards to our will. I've railed against the use of credit cards so vehemently that you might well gasp in shock to hear that I actually advocate their use—although in a very restricted way. Knowing and avoiding the pitfalls of credit cards can clearly outline the danger zones. If we don't cross the red line into the hazard area, then we can tame them, like fire, to provide useful services for us.

What services? Yes, there are indeed good reasons to use a credit card on occasion. One of the best reasons is that it gives you protection in the case of nondelivery of goods or services. If I should buy an autographed first edition of Dr. Seuss's classic *The Cat in the Hat* from my favorite Internet auction site and send the seller a check, I have little or no recourse in the event that the autograph is the seller's and not that of Dr. Seuss. If I pay by credit card, however, the card-issuing company will investigate problems associated with the transaction and have a good chance of recovering some or all of my money.

Some credit cards, in an effort to lure yet more flies into their web of high-interest indebtedness, offer many more perks that can be useful to careful consumers. Some cards offer no-cost additional life insurance to travelers who use their credit card to pay for airline tickets. I know that it would comfort me, during my last seconds while hurtling earthward in some rickety ex-Soviet airliner, to know that Kathy would get a few extra thousand dollars because the ticket was purchased on my Visa card!

Another come-on of actual value are those cards that will double the manufacturer's warranty for products purchased with their cards. The catch is that you, the consumer, must diligently guard paperwork associated with the product: store receipts, credit card receipts, warranty statements, etc. Having some rudimentary filing skills can really make a difference should your new life-size replica of Captain Picard as a Borg drone break down only days after you brought him home from the Sharper Image store.

One of the coolest uses for credit cards comes when you move into that bittersweet phase of life when the children are in college, and astronomical sums flow from your purse into the arms of a hoard of bursars, landlords, bookstores, and everyone else with a hand in educating one's offspring. It comforted me greatly to know that my children's college tuition (and everything else associated with their education) was run through a credit card account that gave me frequent-flier miles on British Airways for every dollar charged. Of course, each month's credit card balance was always immediately paid off in full so that not a dime in interest or penalties ever went to the lending institution.

Every year that my children were in college, their credit card purchases earned enough frequent-flier miles to allow me to take a ministry trip to the former Soviet Union. More recently I've switched to a card that sends vouchers redeemable for ticket purchases on any airline through their special travel agency—a much more flexible solution than one that weds you to a particular airline.

A final reason why judicious use of credit cards can be good for your finances is that they allow you to track expenditures. When we gave each of our college-age children a credit card to be used only in defined situations, such as to pay for course-related books in the bookstore, my son, Josh, immediately began to refer to his card as "Parent in a Pocket"—a term no amount of dissuasion could remove from his vocabulary. Since each child had a different card it was easy to track their educational expenses separately.

My current favorite card, the same one that sends me periodic travel vouchers, also is wonderfully integrated into the financial software package I currently use. Every few days I can download recent expenditures onto my computer, automatically categorize them, and study them for errors and ways to reduce or eliminate them entirely. And if I can't eliminate them, I would prefer to receive travel benefits from them!

Credit cards, like explosives, can be used in a safe and sane manner. The first rule in using them safely is to fear them greatly, for they can destroy your life if you don't bend them to your will.

Budgeting: Keep It Simple

When I took up hang gliding, I was a bit intimidated by the idea of flying an aircraft with no source of power. I soon learned that hang gliders are indeed powered, but it is gravity, not an engine, that enables you to fly from the launch site to the landing field. The catch, though, is to make sure you have enough altitude at any point to get yourself to a suitable landing site.

In one of my early flights I was so excited by the prospect of flying like an eagle that I didn't realize I was also sinking like a brick. It suddenly dawned on me that I had only three options for landing: a field of beehives, a field strewn with power lines, and a field ending in a huge pit bordered with bushes. I opted for the last and was pleased that the only damage suffered by whacking into the bushes was to my pride. I had forgotten that cardinal rule of unpowered flight—to budget my altitude to make sure there's enough to take me to a place of safety.

But really, who wants to think about budgeting anything? Isn't the notion of making a budget about as pleasant as a mouthful of root canals? Actually, the prospect of creating a budget isn't as daunting as the task of following it. When most people think of budgets they immediately lose hope. "If our government can't live within its huge budget, then how can I?" One reason our government can ignore balancing its budget is that the good old USA has inexhaustible credit—so far, at least. But since you and I can't print our own money, we'll need to learn how to squeeze the maximum amount of joy out of every buck.

Let's begin by taking a look at the starting point of any budget—your income. If you follow the general principles I've laid out so far, you will look at the paycheck you get every two weeks (or week or month or whatever), and immediately deduct the 20 percent or so that you will save and give. That means the 80 percent remaining is available to live on. Of course, if you've earmarked 20 or 25 percent for giving and paying off debt, I'm assuming you'll make the necessary adjustments.

Having made those deductions—unless the Lord leads you otherwise—I would advise you to spend the balance. Biblical prudence begins to shade into miserliness when you squirrel away the portion on which you are to live joyfully. The main issue is how to spend it so that you experience both the satisfaction from life that God intended and your bills are paid at the end of the month.

Now let's look at the flip side of a budget—your expenses. I suggest taking a sheet of paper and writing across the top "Available income," followed by the dollar amount that represents 80 percent of your income. Now divide the paper into two columns by drawing a line down the middle of the page. The left side of the page should be called "Fixed Expenses" and the right side "Variable Expenses."

Fixed expenses include the regular payments you must make every month for things like rent or mortgage, utilities, telephone, insurance premiums, etc. These may not be exactly fixed in amount, and we all know that the phone and utility bills can vary. The idea, though, is that these are predictable, nonnegotiable obligations that absolutely must be paid.

What goes on the right side of the page under the heading of variable expenses? Everything else, categorized according to your inclinations. Here are some typical categories: groceries, barber/beauty, clothing, entertainment and dining out, baby-sitter, books and magazines, gas, auto maintenance, home maintenance, and any other category that seems necessary. Try not to have categories that are too specific ("shoes") or too broad ("stuff we need"). This system works best with fewer than a dozen categories.

After a year or two of marriage, Kathy and I added two categories that at the time we called "Ray's Allowance" and "Kathy's Allowance." It may not sound very dignified for adults to have allowances, but the creation of these categories eased a great deal of conflict in our lives.

Our clashes arose out of our differing personalities. Basically, if you remember Aesop's fable about the grasshopper and the ant, the grasshopper had a "Who cares? Live for today!" mentality. On the other hand, the ant was unwilling to do anything but work and save. Well, I'm the grasshopper, and Kathy was the ant. If I felt we needed anything—or if I just *wanted* something!—I would just buy it. Kathy, on the other hand, felt guilty if she even bought a new lipstick. The result was that she was often irritated at my selfishly spending our joint resources while she stoically refused to spend anything on herself.

The creation of these "allowance" categories freed both of us from our entrenched spending patterns. I had a certain amount of money in my "pocket," and when that amount was gone, I found my purchasing power automatically limited. Kathy, though, felt much more free to spend her allotment, and it allowed her to do some impulse purchasing of things she wanted but wouldn't buy prior to the creation of this category.

Couples will find that this is a practical way to avoid some inevitable differences in outlook about each spouse's spending habits. The same tool can be useful for singles, too. Cathy Guisewite's comic-strip character Cathy is a chronic overspender on shoes and accessories for organizing her life. She would benefit greatly from having appropriate budget categories, including a limited personal "allowance!" Even when you don't have to share an income with a spouse, you'll get lifelong benefits from practicing basic budgeting skills.

Once you've finished designing budget categories that work for you, it's time to divide up your available income so that all of the fixed expenses are funded appropriately. This may mean looking over some recent utility and telephone bills so you can arrive at monthly estimates. At first these estimates may be quite a bit off, but you can adjust them later, even recalculating every pay period if you like.

Once you've funded the categories under your fixed expenses, then what's left is available for variable expenses. In order to arrive at educated estimates to plug into each of the categories you've designated as variable, you will need to keep track for a month or two of your expenditures on gasoline, health and beauty products, groceries, etc. (Of course, this may be an eye-opening experience that will immediately suggest some adjustments you'll want to make in your budget for the future.) Complete the process until all of the expense categories on both sides of the sheet are funded, and the total matches the available income. Then you can begin turning your budget—which is, after all, only a written plan—into reality.

As usual, planning is a lot easier than implementing! But implementing a simple budget is much less painful than adopting a complicated one that requires lots of recording, analysis, or forecasting. That's why I think it's essential that your budget process be kept simple, or at least start that way. So far it's a single sheet of paper that adds up to the amount that God has provided for you to live joyfully in the here and now. In the next chapter I'll suggest some practical ways you can translate that piece of paper into a spending plan in action.

Chapter 21

The Envelope System

What peace and harmony the single document described in the previous chapter can bring to a family! That simple sheet of paper brought Kathy and me together to work out our spending priorities. For the first time I realized that she had a thrifty antlike nature and that I was just a free-spending grasshopper at heart. As we made a common commitment to our spending, I realized that we had made a giant step toward better communication as a couple, but we still had to implement an actual method of spending according to our written priorities. That method was the discovery of the envelope system, which automatically managed our spending on variable expenses.

Here's how it works. Let's assume that each pay period your paycheck is automatically deposited to your checking account (if it's not, you might as well get that rolling). Let's say it's deposited on the first and the fifteenth of every month in equal amounts. On payday, you write checks on your account to cover your regular monthly fixed expenses, like housing and insurance. Since my mortgage payment was always huge compared to everything else, and was due on the sixth of the month, I would always pay that from my first paycheck of the month. All other fixed expenses came from the second paycheck.

Then you look at your one-page budget to total your variable expenses for the pay period. Let's assume that total is $600. Go to the bank and cash a check for $600, being sure to get a good assortment of five- and one-dollar bills.

To implement the envelope system, you will need to buy some sturdy Ziploc bags, preferably something like the plastic zippered envelopes that are sold for keeping pencils and the like in a loose-leaf binder. Get as many envelopes as you have variable categories (and a couple extra for new categories), label them, and fill each envelope with the amount of cash designated for that category. If you get the kind of plastic envelope made for notebook organizers, you might consider a zippered binder to hold them all together.

The beauty of this system is that, when followed, it automatically prevents overspending. What happens when the groceries envelope is empty? You have a choice—spend nothing on groceries until the next pay period or use money from another category. Yes, you can do that! This system is not a dictatorial tyrant—YOU are the boss. Of course, if the only category left is "gas" and you don't want to walk for a week, or there's money in "entertainment and dining out" but there's a new restaurant you want to try this week, you may decide to simply live on leftovers for a few days.

I once worked closely with an associate whose family always seemed to be on the edge of financial disaster. He earned about the same amount that I did and wasn't a conspicuous consumer, so I suggested that he consider the budget system that Kathy and I had found so helpful.

Boy, did I hit a nerve! He believed that he was an expert on budgets. It turned out that he had a pocket notebook in which every cent he spent was recorded, and this in turn was recorded in a myriad of ways on his computer. He could produce tables and graphs showing the precise expenditure of every nickel he had earned for years!

What he didn't understand is that keeping track of expenditures after the fact has little to do with living within a budget. The whole point of budgeting is to control spending in real time, not retroactively account for it all. My friend approached budgeting the way a crash-analysis expert would deal with flying: He may have never flown a plane, but he could tell you exactly what went wrong in every crash!

The envelope system forces you to do your numerical work *before* you spend your money, not afterward. Of course, as your knowledge about your expenses grows, you may refine the way you fund your categories, and this has a wonderful effect in training you to live within your income.

For example, some people have grown up unconscious of the cost of electricity, telephone, and groceries. I know I did. My parents paid for everything, and while my father was forever going around turning off lights, I figured electricity didn't cost much.

Yet when you study that latest electricity bill, and note that if you could just reduce it by $20 you would have enough to increase the funding of the "entertainment and dining out" envelope, you become truly motivated! You begin to turn lights out. You look for coupons for oil changes. You seek out bulk staples in the grocery store and avoid costly frozen entrées. You discover that a backyard garden can save $50 per month in groceries, and it's even fun to grow. You realize that there are such things as $2 movie theaters, and libraries don't charge for letting you borrow books.

The envelope system does present what could be considered some pitfalls. One risk is that of being robbed or losing your envelope stash. While this is a real possibility, the costs of not implementing a functional budget are lifelong and much greater! Another pitfall in some people's minds is that in order to use this system you will have to plan ahead (what a concept!). When you go out you'll have to have the appropriate envelope with you. If you forget, you will immediately be tempted to write a check, or—more likely—put your purchase on a credit card. You'll be tempted to rationalize it: "When the card statement comes in I'll be sure to even things out." Will you really?

Perhaps once you master the envelope system and get plenty of practice tracking and limiting your spending, you could consider keeping an index card in each envelope instead of the allotment of cash. Instead of placing $40 in cash in the "barber and beauty" envelope, the sum of $40 is penciled in on the index card and the actual expense is placed on a credit card. Immediately after each purchase, you would record the exact expenditure on the appropriate index card and deduct it from the balance, stopping all expenditures in that category when the balance approached zero. This method puts a choke chain around the neck of the credit card. But only if you are very disciplined and careful can you combine the advantages of the envelope system with the convenience of a credit card. Rookies would be wise to use the cash envelopes for a year before making major adjustments.

Another positive aspect of the envelope system is that it allows for cash to build up in some envelopes over time. Auto maintenance is a prime example. As you fund that category each month, if you're lucky you'll just pay for routine oil changes. The rest of the cash will grow untouched until you actually need to dip into it for more major expenses such as new tires or a timing belt. In fact, if you are so blessed as to not experience major breakdowns, a time might come where it doesn't make sense to keep all that money in an envelope, and you should consider opening an interest-bearing bank account or a mutual fund account dedicated to auto maintenance. Believe me, when the day comes that somebody says, "Well, mister, this transmission has had it!" you'll be glad you didn't rob *that* envelope to squeeze another dining-out experience from your budget!

When you begin using this system you'll experience the usual degree of start-up difficulties involved in learning any new discipline. Don't give up! By all means give this system a fair try—at least six months. Begin to gather information on your fixed and variable expenses. Buy envelopes you like that will last a long time. From time to time you'll get some strange looks from checkout clerks, but you can have the satisfaction of knowing that you're in control of your finances and that joyfully living within your means has become a reality.

Chapter 22

Computerizing Your Finances

Of all my childhood chores, the one I most despised was mowing the lawn. Not only did we not have a power mower (nobody did), but the sheer drudgery of pushing that mower up and down the hilly yards of northern Kentucky did nothing but sap my spirit. So I passed the time daydreaming about the future. I *knew* what the future would be like: monorails, personal jetpacks, helicoptering to work or college, vacations on the moon. They were all as clear to my mind's eye as the cover of *Amazing Stories* or *Science Fiction Magazine*. I imagined robot-guided self-powered lawn mowers that would do my outdoor chores or, even better, a robot that could also clean the basement or even—ugh—dig holes for my gardening-obsessed grandmother.

Somehow the personal jetpacks never made it to the consumer mainstream, and the future is decidedly different than imagined in those science-fiction magazines of my youth. On the other hand, I never dreamed that I would have intelligent mechanical helpers assisting me in managing my personal finances! The future has brought with it miraculous machines—computers—that can be used to ease all the tasks related to managing the financial resources God has given us.

As I described my paperless budget (the envelope system), an insightful reader might have noticed that I tend to opt for simple solutions. I am, in fact, one of the laziest individuals you will ever meet. I do everything possible to make life easy and convenient. Sometimes my family is irritated to no end by the pains I'll take in the pursuit of automating otherwise simple tasks, but it's my nature. I hate paying bills about as much as mowing the lawn. As far as balancing checkbooks or other financial accounts—I hate that, too. The person writing these pages is not some wannabe accountant who is never happier than when surrounded by ledgers and statements. If I could, I would avoid the whole thing.

That all changed, however, with the advent of personal finance programs that would actually print checks that only needed to be signed and stuffed into a special window envelope for mailing. Suddenly, the advantages of a computerized checkbook began to make sense, especially because the software remembered payments, addresses, and did other tasks that actually made the whole job easier.

Computerized personal finance made another huge leap when on-line check-writing services became available. Now there are several, and most of them work in the same way. When you set up your checking account to work with one of these check-writing services, you simply fill out an on-screen form. You enter the payee, amount, date, a budget category, etc. The program usually offers to fill in data from the last check written to that payee, making things much simpler. When you have written all the checks, the computer sends the data off electronically via a phone call (or Internet connection) to the check-writing company. The company makes an electronic transfer to the payee wherever possible (such as to the gas company, the phone company, etc.) or mails a printed check in an envelope if direct payment isn't possible.

The advantage for the savvy computer user is not so much a savings of time and effort, but the fact that expenses paid in this way can be so easily recorded and tracked. Modern personal finance software can give you incredibly useful reports in seconds. What did I spend on utilities this year? Last year? How much went for groceries or automobile repairs? Best of all, these programs can tell you in seconds whether or not you are achieving your goals for giving or saving. "Be sure you know the condition of your flocks, give careful attention to your herds," says Proverbs 27:23. Part of wise financial management is keeping your finger on the pulse of your income, expenses, giving, and saving. Nothing makes this more painless than a computer and appropriate software.

If you keep your savings and investment data in the program, and it really makes sense to do so, there are additional benefits. Most programs are designed to price an investment portfolio (i.e., a collection of stocks or mutual funds) via a brief connection to the Internet. The one I use goes even further: It synchronizes the financial data on my computer with the investment accounts I have with major brokerage firms. In seconds it can update my records and know within a few dollars the value of each account.

Of course, this knowledge brings with it certain temptations. It makes you more aware of your assets and whether they are shrinking or growing. Either way can cause you to lose sight of the big picture. Remember, this is God's money, not yours. If it is growing, praise God but remember that it is his, and he may have a plan for it other than whatever you might like to buy with it. If it is dwindling due to market vagaries, don't worry—it's his money, and he has more. Your job is to manage it faithfully, neither rapaciously nor lazily.

Speaking of lazy, my favorite use for personal finance software is to download data from credit cards and bank accounts. I can reconcile a credit card statement in minutes, concluding with a single click that orders an electronic transfer to pay the balance. If I were starting my financial life from scratch, I would choose only institutions (banking, credit card, investment firms) that allow transactions to be downloaded into my personal finance software of choice. Many banks and other institutions offer on-line access to account data through the Internet, typically by means of a World Wide Web browser such as Internet Explorer or Netscape Navigator. This is a very second-class way to access one's personal finances. These days I *insist* that accounts I use frequently be directly compatible with my software.

If you don't want to own a computer, and the envelope system of budgeting works well for you, stick with it! My motto is, the simpler the better. But if computerizing your finances appeals to you for the reasons I've described, then by all means buy some good personal finance software.

Don't worry too much about your computer itself being state-of-the-art. Will it do what you want it to do? If you want to do word processing, Internet browsing, and run financial software, any mainstream computer less than two years old should do fine. Here's a good strategy: Find the software you want to run, look at the back of the box and note the minimum requirements. Let that be your starting point when shopping for a computer. If you do this, then you will be sure that you can run the programs you need the computer for, and you'll be perfectly satisfied with a used computer that you can purchase for a fraction of the price of a new one. Don't get sidetracked by the glitzy new machines! It's very easy to catch a disease closely related to new-car fever. Buy for utility, and don't try to buy a computer for the next decade. It's enough to get through the next two to three years.

Remember the reason for having a computer to track your finances in the first place: to help you ride herd on your "sheep" and have an up-to-date and accurate understanding of the state of your flocks. Computers are only tools, yet they have assisted me greatly in my pursuit of managing God's assets in ways that will be pleasing to him. And they're fun to play with until the personal jet-packs arrive!

Chapter 23

Insurance Dos and Don'ts

We've already talked at some length about how investing is a way of setting aside a portion of what God provides today to meet probable future needs. Buying insurance is a way of setting aside a portion of what God provides today to meet possible future needs. Phrased this way, you can see that they are very similar, and prudence would require that most Christians take advantage of both.

However, in light of what I said earlier about the temptation to trust in wealth rather than God to protect us from disaster, you may wonder if insurance demonstrates a lack of faith in God. Some would say yes, that insuring one's life or property is an attempt to usurp God's ultimate control of the universe. I don't think they're right. On the other hand, people are often targeted by insurance salesmen who proceed to sell them a great deal of costly and unnecessary coverage. The balance, as usual, is somewhere in between.

Anyone who might oppose the purchase of insurance on the basis of its unavailability in biblical times has a point. But remember that zippers and air travel were equally unavailable. The concept of insurance is based on prudence and bearing each other's burdens, both thoroughly biblical concepts. The theory is that many people can each contribute a little bit to a common fund, and when a disaster overtakes any member of the group, the fund is available to meet the financial aspects of the disaster. Of course, standardized units of wealth (money) hadn't even been invented until the sixth century before Christ (although wealth has always been with us), but the concept of being a part of a larger group or tribe has always been an important aspect of the human family.

Long before King Croesus stamped the first coins, the author of Ecclesiastes wrote: "Two are better than one, because they have a good return for their work: If one falls down, his friend can help him up. But pity the man who falls and has no one to help him up! Also, if two lie down together, they will keep warm. But how can one keep warm alone? Though one may be overpowered, two can defend themselves. A cord of three strands is not quickly broken" (Ecclesiastes 4:9-12). The common thread in these verses is that there is safety in numbers. Just as mountain climbers rope themselves together for mutual safety, insurance is a way of joining with others in similar situations so that if one falls off the cliff, the others will see that he is pulled to safety well before he hits the rocks below.

Once you decide if buying insurance is right for you and your family, the picture gets complicated by the fact that there are many kinds of insurance. The most common types of modern insurance include home and property, life, health, and auto.

When you buy a house, you'll need insurance that will protect both you and the mortgage lender in the case of fire, flood, earthquake, or other disasters. And renters should seriously consider purchasing renter's insurance. If you're robbed, the insurance could help replace your most important possessions. If you've furnished your apartment in thrift-shop contemporary, you might want to weigh the cost of renter's insurance versus the cost of replacing your stuff with another visit to the Goodwill store. However, if you possess some real valuables, such as antiques, art, or coins, you should definitely not only get renter's insurance, but make sure that your valuables are appropriately recorded and appraised. Most property insurance policies would not cover such valuable items unless you take steps to make sure your ownership of them is documented.

But so what if you lose all your material possessions—you still have your health, right? Not necessarily, and the funds you might need to take care of future health problems are a great reason to look into health insurance. If you're employed by a large company, you may be fortunate enough to have a good health insurance plan that is a part of your total compensation package. If so, take the time and effort to struggle through the details of your health plan. You need to find out what is covered, when, and what prior authorization may be required for specific medical procedures.

If health insurance is available as a benefit of your employment, definitely take it. If it is not, do a risk-benefit analysis regarding purchasing your own health insurance policy. If you're young and healthy and not a part of some employee health plan, it might be wiser to rely on your own "self-funded" health plan. In other words, pay for your own checkups, shots, and occasional visits to the urgent-care clinic out of your well-funded "cushion." Then supplement this do-it-yourself coverage with a major medical health plan with a high deductible. This kind of plan may cost only a few hundred dollars per year and could save your bacon if you encounter major medical expenses, such as those associated with a premature baby or a lengthy hospital stay.

In general, it is always better to try to join some sort of group when seeking health insurance since insurers can assess their financial risks with a group much better than with a single individual. In any case, if you decide you need it, shop around! Your goal should be to pay the least while buying protection against a major calamity. You can save enough to buy all the aspirin you need out of your own pocket!

Health insurance can only work up to a point—eventually we all die. And that's where life insurance enters the picture. Life insurance pays those who are left behind after the days God has given you have expired. How much life insurance is appropriate?

Before you decide to buy life insurance, ask yourself whether you need it at all. For many young singles or couples, it just isn't necessary. The picture changes when children come along. If one spouse dies, the other needs enough money to continue to raise the children without having to work twenty-four hours a day.

If you decide to buy life insurance, be sure you understand what it is designed to do. Insurance is not some kind of lottery where the death of a spouse means the other needn't work for life! Of course, sometimes life insurance policies are included as a part of a total employment compensation package and represent a fringe benefit that can't reasonably be turned down. But if you're paying hard-earned money out of your disposable income, you'll want to buy the least that will do the job.

All too often naive consumers buy insurance that has been aggressively touted as an investment. It works like this: You pay your premiums, and if you die your beneficiary is paid the full value of the policy. If you don't die, the insurance company pays you back much more than you paid into the company through your premiums, usually at age sixty-five or some other predetermined date. It sounds like a "no lose" proposition, doesn't it?

This kind of policy is known as whole life insurance, so called because it "covers" you in either death or life. It is, in fact, a no-win situation. In order to make this clear, let me contrast term insurance with whole life insurance. If you buy a $100,000 term life insurance policy at age thirty, you might pay $300 each year, but the amount goes up each year as your risk of dying increases with age. If you buy a similar whole life policy, you might pay $800 each year, but that premium amount would never increase.

If you live to age sixty-five, and keep your policy in force by paying your premiums, the term life policy pays nothing—unless you die, that is. The whole life policy, however, has accumulated a "cash value." During the course of the policy you can borrow against this cash value (but not cheaply!), and when the policy matures, you might be rewarded with a hefty check or possibly annual payments for life.

In effect, whole life insurance is an insurance policy combined with a forced-savings plan. You pay a fixed amount each year— much more than is actually required by the insurance company to fund death benefits—and the difference is invested by the company in standard investment vehicles of its own choosing, such as stocks, mutual funds, or real estate. If you don't die, the amount they pay you when the policy matures is very much *less* than the company hopes to make through its investments. In other words, you would be much better off simply buying term insurance and maintaining your own investment portfolio. The bottom line: When you buy life insurance, it should be primarily for your family's financial protection in the event of your untimely death, not as an integral component of some half-baked investment scheme.

Insurance, like a parachute, had better be there when you need it. The purchase of some kinds of insurance is optional—it's up to you to set aside against an improbable future catastrophe. Automobile liability insurance, on the other hand, is not an option. You must buy and maintain at least the legal minimums of liability insurance required in your state. The consequences for failure to do so can be extremely serious. In the event of an accident for which you are found liable, you could be subject to a legal judgment that could haunt you for years and cripple your ability to save and acquire the assets you and your family will need.

This situation is surely governed by Jesus' statement of the Golden Rule: "Do unto others as you would have them do unto you." If you would like others to be insured, then you need to be insured. Liability insurance has one essential purpose: If you are ever held accountable for some huge financial judgment, the insurance company will shield you up to the dollar limits of the policy. It will do this by paying whatever is required or by defending you in court. The choice is up to the insurer, and it generally means that you needn't hire an attorney to defend yourself against lawsuits, whether well-founded or fraudulent.

An important consideration when buying liability insurance is how much you're getting for your money. The legal minimums that most states require you to carry are fairly low, but liability judgments can be huge. You need to assess whether or not a liability limit of $25,000, $100,000, or even more might be appropriate. Surprisingly, liability insurance does not cost a great deal more for the higher policy limits. In any case, select from a company that has recently received high ratings from the Consumers Union or the equivalent. All insurance companies are certainly not equal when it comes to customer satisfaction.

When buying liability insurance, you may want to consider other options on your automobile policy, the most common being collision, comprehensive, and uninsured motorist supplements. Collision pays for the repair or replacement of your car in case of an accident, while comprehensive covers loss from most causes, the most important of which is theft. Finally, uninsured motorist covers you and your passengers in the event you are involved in an accident with someone who does not carry the proper insurance—a very likely scenario in most states.

Last week one of Josh's friends called him with a terrible story of being hit by an uninsured—and drunk—motorist, who wrecked Josh's friend's truck and left him and his passenger liable for all of their medical expenses. Josh's friend had *thought* that his policy covered uninsured motorists, but he was out of luck.

In general, the options mentioned above cost more—sometimes much more—than basic liability coverage. If your car is reasonably new, it might be wise to carry collision and comprehensive coverage, but even then the premium can be dramatically reduced by carrying a high deductible, such as $500. If your car were totaled, you would be paid the value of the car (according to the insurance company's valuation, which probably won't agree with what the car was worth to you!), less the deductible. If you were involved in a minor fender bender and your total damages were only $400, then you would pay it all out of your pocket, but if the damage totaled $550, the insurance company would at least kick in $50.

One of my seminary students drove a twelve-year-old Volkswagen Beetle. One day I heard the distressing news that it had been stolen from the parking space at his apartment, and when I called to console him, he astounded me by saying it was fully insured. The insurance company eventually paid him $2,000. Based on what I knew about the cost of insurance, I concluded that he was paying as much as $400 per year for that comprehensive coverage. Using the same investment assumptions as I used in the millionaire janitor story in chapter 15, he could have amassed that much just by investing $400 each year for four years. He would have been much better off having a large deductible and saving the difference. Of course, since he apparently had no liquid cushion, the loss of his car would have been calamitous, so he had to take the insurance route.

If you have savings such that the loss of a car is not catastrophic, then you are probably better off sticking with only liability insurance plus uninsured motorist, which isn't very expensive and provides a great deal of coverage for your passengers. In any event, find out what you would pay for additional coverage and ask yourself if you couldn't do better by "self-insuring" through your savings.

Remember the main purpose of insurance—it's to provide a way to anticipate and offset the impact of truly catastrophic losses. For Christians, it's appropriate to make plans to deal with the most likely reversals in life, but we also need to remember what the psalmist wrote: "The LORD is my rock, my fortress and my deliverer; my God is my rock, in whom I take refuge. He is my shield and the horn of my salvation, my stronghold" (Psalm 18:2). Only the Lord can truly shield us from disaster. We can be confident that anything that he allows into our lives has been carefully screened through the grid of his great love.

To Rent or to Buy?

"Be it ever so humble, there's no place like home!" Most of us have a home, but few are as humble as the one occupied by my friend Roy Rosedale while working as an agricultural aid worker in India. It was made of sticks with a straw roof, and when the floor got really dirty he had a lady come in from the nearby village and lay down a fresh, smooth layer of cow dung!

Actually, that hut was probably reasonably well adapted to life in a rural Indian village. The challenge for us is to find housing that is economically appropriate and yet meets our needs for a secure, clean roof over our heads. Should we rent or should we buy? How much rent (or mortgage payment) is appropriate for our income?

Underlying these questions is the issue (never far away in this book) of choosing one's lifestyle rather than falling by default into an inappropriate spending pattern. You have a great deal of discretion in selecting your housing, and your choices will help determine one of any number of possible financial futures. Unless you are committed to living well within your income and saving the surplus, you may find that you don't have any choice—your only option will be to rent indefinitely.

Renting, however, actually has many advantages, especially for young people. When you're just starting out in adult life you may try different jobs, even different careers. You may have to relocate to different parts of the country every few years. When you're new in a city, you may not know where you'd like to buy until you understand the dynamics of your new situation. Through renting you also can try out many types of homes: town houses, apartments, duplexes, single-family homes, lofts, converted industrial buildings—you name it, people have made housing out of it. If you rent, you can sample from this smorgasbord of housing options and figure out what you do and don't like.

Renting also allows you flexibility in your housing budget. If your income shrinks or you're temporarily unemployed, you can easily downsize and make your savings cushion last longer. Homeowners who are laid off (and without savings) can face foreclosure in only a few months. This is the situation reflected in the oft-repeated (but poorly documented) political slogan that holds that "70 percent of Americans are only a paycheck away from losing their homes."

Finally, renting is a way to preserve your assets during times when property values are falling. Almost everybody born after World War II believes that housing is a gold-plated investment and that real estate values never go down. Many Californians have found that there is no such guarantee, and numerous homeowners who bought in the late 1980s or early 1990s saw the value of their homes plummet. Renters, on the other hand, did just fine during those years. In fact, during times when the cost of buying a home has hit record levels, renting has sometimes become a bargain.

Kathy and I started our married life while I was in the air force, and we were provided free government housing at our tiny military base in Cambria. Since we didn't have to pay rent, we were especially aggressive about saving during those years. When we left the air force and joined the staff of Campus Crusade for Christ, our first assignment was in Tampa, Florida. We arrived in early September and eagerly began to seek out a house to meet our needs and our budget. My ministry director had just bought a nice house in a new neighborhood and encouraged us to live in the same area. We soon determined that what would be best for our budget was a much older house for a much lower price.

We believe the Lord led us to rent a faded old bungalow near the dog track but next door to a lovely older Christian lady who remained a friend until she passed away years later. The house had a porch, a dining room (important, as Kathy had bought a prized oak dining room set before our marriage), and enough bedrooms so that we could have an office and someday a baby's room. To top it off, there was a solar water heater!

This was not the perfect house, mind you. The paint was peeling, and there were some bouncy places (especially in the kitchen) that caused one to wonder if the floor had springs like a trampoline. The house was just a block from a tacky commercial street lined with bars and pawn shops. When Kathy's parents came down to visit us, her dad obviously disliked our choice and forcefully expressed the view that he had spent his whole life trying to get away from houses and neighborhoods like the one we had selected for our home.

The valuable insight we drew from my father-in-law's comment was that his housing career had begun somewhere near the same level as ours. It was only after years of labor as a successful highway contractor that he was able to provide the higher level of housing that Kathy and her family had enjoyed for so many years!

Kathy and I weren't partners in a highway contracting firm—and it didn't seem likely that we would ever be able to afford a house as nice as the one her parents had bought. Still, we did want to own a home of our own someday. That meant we would have to be even more frugal when renting if homeownership was to be feasible sometime down the road.

As we look back now, we are so glad that we chose an appropriate lifestyle (and house) for us rather than bowing to the expectations of others. We had many happy times in that rented house and many others in the house that we were able to buy because of the money we saved by that early housing choice.

My recently married nephew and his new bride settled in Southern California and took jobs in an area notorious for the exorbitant cost of housing. Rather than invest a high percentage of their income in housing, they sought and found an opportunity to live rent-free in a small guesthouse in exchange for doing house- and yard work. They had to work a few hours a week, but the money they saved in only a year allowed them to make a significant down payment on a new house, one they never could have afforded if they had not chosen wisely in the beginning.

Steeped as most of us are in the notion that we should live as high on the hog as possible, it may be difficult to make wise entry-level housing choices. The thing we must always remember is that while saving involves deferred gratification, the gratification usually will come one day if we save. If we don't, our housing choices narrow because of a lack of an appropriate down payment.

I have stressed the positive values of renting and am convinced that it represents a much underrated housing solution. But the fact remains that homeownership has historically been a winning investment, so renting wisely in the beginning can open the doors to affordable homeownership later. In the next chapter I'll change my tune and explore the benefits of being the master of one's castle.

Chapter 25

Home Sweet Home

Ever since I can remember I've despised cockroaches above all living creatures. At an early and impressionable age I was once terrorized by a huge flying cockroach that seemed intent on homing in on my face, and the aversion has spread to our family. Our first week living in the Philippines, my daughter, Laurie, felt a cockroach drop into her hair from the ceiling of a Manila restaurant. Her resulting screams froze the blood of an entire restaurant full of diners.

One of the unhappy surprises we discovered in our inexpensive Tampa rental was cockroaches. And the house didn't have just a few roaches, but platoons and battalions of them! At night we would sneak down the darkened hall and throw on the kitchen light. Massive quantities of insect life would scurry toward the nearest crack, and I (with Kathy cheering me on from a position of safety) would go into a stomping frenzy until every roach had either made its escape or been converted to a squish mark on the aging linoleum floor.

While a nasty fact of life in Florida, the roaches weren't a problem for our landlady—but the termites were. Only a few months after we moved in we noticed that the refrigerator seemed to be sagging strangely, as though the floor beneath had turned to rubber. Not long afterward we came home from campus to find termites by the millions swarming throughout the house! Our landlady had no choice but to have the whole house tented and fumigated. To our delight, this also dealt with the roach problem.

Every time we were tempted to knock our rented house, we remembered that God had led us to it. We reminded ourselves that we had deliberately chosen a low-cost lifestyle so that we might have our own house someday. The savings we enjoyed by living in our rental allowed us to continue to save aggressively for a home. Meanwhile, we avoided all the financial duties of homeowning. After all, the expenses of fumigating for termites and repairing the kitchen floor fell on our landlady, not us. At last, we left Tampa and had accumulated a significant sum designated for a down payment on a home of our own.

In chapter 17, I warned against the dangers of indebtedness. There are few legitimate reasons why one would voluntarily shackle oneself to debt, but I believe that buying a home is one of them. In rising housing markets it is a definite advantage to be able to buy a house here and now with borrowed money rather than have to save for decades to be able to buy one with cash.

The downside, of course, to buying a home through a home mortgage is that the vast bulk of your payments is interest to the lender. For example, if you borrowed $100,000 to buy a home at 8 percent interest to be paid back monthly for thirty years, your loan payment (not counting taxes, insurance, etc.) would be $733.36. How much of that first payment is interest on the loan? Most of it!

In fact, $667 would be interest, or more than 90 percent of your house payment. Over time you gradually begin paying back more principle and less interest, but even at the ten-year point your payments are almost 80 percent interest.

Let's say that you sell the house after ten years. You would have paid 120 monthly payments of $733.36, for a total outlay of $88,000. Now, a portion of each payment went to pay back the loan, and this is called "building equity" in the house. But after ten years, the amount you would have to pay the lender to pay off the mortgage would be $77,725. That means that only $12,125 of the original loan amount was paid off with your payments of $88,000! That sounds like a pretty lousy deal. Why pay $88,000 in order to build an equity of $12,125?

One aspect that might improve the appearance of such a housing investment is the hope that the house might rise in value over those ten years. If it does, that increase in value increases your equity in the house. If the value of the house has doubled, it is now worth $200,000. If you sold it after ten years you would pay the lender $87,725, but would receive the balance of the $200,000. Your net profit: $112,225.

This is why many people buy houses—they assume (and usually correctly) that the property value will go up, and their house will provide both a place to live as well as a marvelous investment. These were the assumptions of our Realtor and mortgage lender when Kathy and I began hunting for our first home. We knew what our income was, how much we had in assets, and how much of that we were willing to put into a down payment on a house. This meant that we could afford to buy a house under a certain amount and not more. However, we experienced a great deal of pressure to spend more than we could afford.

Our Realtor began by taking us to house after house that was well out of our price range. No conceivable haggling could bring any of these homes down to an attainable level. We met resistance when we asked to see houses in our price range. We were told that there just weren't any on the market at the price we were willing to pay. Our Realtor and mortgage lender both felt "sure" that housing prices would continue to rise, and that our income would also continue to rise. Their belief was that one should always buy as much house as the lender would qualify him to borrow. But is this approach sound?

A coworker recently told me that he received an inheritance six years ago and used it toward the purchase of a house. Unfortunately, he bought at the very top of the real estate market, and his house is now worth about $40,000 less than what he paid for it. He has made mortgage payments for six years, but his equity in the house is still negative. He is in the hole for about $30,000. In other words, his investment resulted in losing his inheritance as well as earning him a boatload of debt.

Like all investments, investing in a house is not a surefire winner. Borrowing to buy a house is a risk, not automatic money in the bank. I write these things not to scare the daylights out of you, but to give you a clear view of the potential perils of home-mortgage debt.

So why would anyone want to buy a home? you might be wondering. *It sounds much safer to rent.* Yes, there is a measure of safety and flexibility in renting, but there are benefits to owning your house. You can freely improve your home, personalizing it in a way that renters cannot. You can deduct the interest portion of your mortgage payment from your income taxes, and that's a huge deduction for young mortgages. And a well-situated house is much more likely to appreciate than not. It's possible to accumulate a good chunk of equity in your home, which can serve you well when you sell it. If you aren't planning to stay put for at least five years, however, it might not be a good idea to buy at all because the costs associated with buying and maintaining a home usually only prove worthwhile as your property appreciates over time.

When Kathy and I concluded that the time to buy a starter home had come, we didn't plan to move for at least four years, and the housing market in central Indiana was very stable. Fortunately, we resisted the pressure we got from our Realtor and stayed within our target price range. We bought a house that pleased us enormously—even though our Realtor and our relatives were not impressed! We could afford to pay the principal, taxes, insurance, and utilities out of the "live joyfully" part of our income and continue to give and save as we had all along. And even when buying our first house we were never without that three-month-savings cushion.

We've owned several homes since that first one, and we've never deviated from our policy of determining an affordable level of housing within the 80 percent of our income we've designated for living costs. Many homeowners, however, will save for a house while they are renting but stop saving when they buy their first house. It's not hard to figure out why: They bought more house than they could afford. Then there is no option but to put 30 to 50 percent of their income into the house, not to mention taxes, insurance, utilities, etc. Often those in this situation can't make repairs, let alone improvements, because of their overbuying. You've probably heard the expression "house-poor," meaning that the house eats up more than its share of financial resources.

Giving also becomes difficult under these circumstances. One pastor I know laments the fact that many of the members of his church bought huge new homes in a prestigious suburb nearby (at the peak of the housing market, I might add) and are so strapped for cash that their giving has been far from what it should be. Doesn't this describe the scenario of taking all that God has provided and making it "ours?" Homeownership should be a blessing from God, not an excuse to squander his resources.

We may have far grander homes than my friend who lived in the hut with the dung floor, but do we live in peace and financial freedom? If we're living so close to the financial edge that we fear losing our house, then the answer is obvious. Too many people make homeownership a curse by choosing housing at a level inappropriate to the income God has given them.

So do some realistic thinking about housing. Ruthlessly examine your wants, your needs, your goals, and your income. What expectations are realistic and in keeping with whatever lifestyle God has called you to enjoy?

Housing is important, but it isn't everything. Proverbs 17:1 advises, "Better a dry crust with peace and quiet than a house full of feasting, with strife." The surest way to destroy your peace is by worries derived from poor choices in housing. If necessary, rent modestly now, save aggressively, buy wisely later, and enjoy greatly!

Chapter 26

Deals on Wheels

Is there anything more wonderful than the smell of the interior of a new car? I know well the lure of new-car fever. One day I decided to drop in on a dealer's showroom, "just to see what they're selling these days." After a while I was picking up brochures and studying lists of available options. I found myself wondering if the extra insulation option might not be a good idea. On the way home I stopped at the supermarket, where I began to browse through the car magazines, and—well, then it was too late. I had contracted a five-alarm case of new-car fever. And it all started with a single whiff of new-car smell!

From a purely financial point of view, it almost always makes sense to buy a used rather than new car. But "You are what you drive," they say, and every car salesman knows that the key to making a sale is to deduce what image the customer wants to project. It's easy to be seduced by the image of yourself wheeling through the neighborhood in the latest convertible or sport utility vehicle.

Car ownership has nearly as many pitfalls as homeownership, and the financial ramifications of poor choices made here can haunt you for decades. Some of the most common unwise financial moves people make when it comes to buying automobiles include buying new when used would do, borrowing in order to buy, and leasing.

Perhaps you don't like the idea of buying a used car. Many people believe that it's safer to buy a new car. It comes with a warranty, and new cars shouldn't need major repairs (transmission rebuilds, major brake jobs, new ball joints, etc.) until it's time to trade the car for another new car. In fact, many people trade their cars every three years so that the manufacturers' warranty will always be in effect. "Why buy somebody else's problems?" is the way this philosophy is often expressed.

The short answer is, "Buying someone else's used problems is much cheaper than buying your own brand-new ones!" For example, let's assume that somebody bought a new car for $17,000 and sold it after two years for the current market value of $8,500. Note that they lost half the value of the car in the first two years to depreciation at the rate of $354 per month! Then they presumably bought another new car, and continued on their merry way tossing cash into the depreciation Dumpster. Does this make financial sense? Had the owners instead bought a used car for $6,000 and saved that $354 per month in depreciation, they could have afforded a new transmission every three months or a new engine every six months.

But does buying a new car make sense from the reliability point of view? After all, there's nothing less appealing than the prospect of finding oneself stranded by the side of the freeway some dark and stormy night. Even here, though, new cars don't always deliver as reliably as used. While cars with fifty to a hundred thousand miles on them are more likely than new cars to need major repairs, they aren't much more likely to fail suddenly, especially if they are regularly maintained.

That's a key, by the way. If you take good care of your vehicle, you won't eliminate the possibility of significant expenses, but if you ignore scheduled maintenance you will very possibly destroy the whole machine. Remember that your car, like everything else, is ultimately God's property. What level of maintenance does that imply? If you've been faithful to live within your income, you should have enough reserves to deal with the occasional unexpected car expense, especially if you've been allowing your "auto maintenance" envelope to grow.

One of the most important questions when it comes to buying a car is hardly ever asked. "Should you pay cash or borrow?" So few people pay cash (drug dealers excepted) that car dealers are often startled when you don't care about finance terms. Almost all car advertising is predicated on the idea that the buyer will be borrowing, so the "price" is usually given in terms of a monthly payment.

The advantages of paying cash, however, are enormous. Remember, money invested builds up rapidly over time, thanks to the miracle of compounding. The flip side is that it takes a lot more money to buy a car through borrowing. The difference between the two is often enough to buy another car!

But how could I possibly pay cash for a car? you're probably wondering. Well, think it through with me. Several years ago, Kathy and I were very impressed with the new crop of minivans that had hit the market. We felt that a minivan would be perfect for hauling the children's soccer teams around, etc., and we made plans to buy one in three to four years. We did two things that made it possible to fulfill that desire despite our typically slim "missionary" salary.

First, we set up an automatic transfer of $300 per month from our checking account to a car savings fund. Once our account was set up we didn't have to do anything except be sure that we didn't overspend. The envelope system helped control our spending so that we didn't get ourselves into debt while siphoning off $300 we were used to living on each month.

Later we confided to some friends how we had set up that automatic transfer to fund our car purchase. They were shocked— how could we live with a $300 cut in our living expenses? The irony was that this couple was planning to take on an even larger monthly car payment, but they didn't seem to see that as a significant problem! (Bottom line: If you can't afford to save the equivalent of a car payment each month, then you probably shouldn't consider buying a car.)

The money we were saving went directly into a highly rated mutual fund that gave us a better return on our investment than a bank savings account would have. We deliberately chose a fairly aggressive fund for our car-savings plan, as we were convinced that market fluctuations might actually help our case. When the market was down, our $300 bought more shares than normal, and when the market was up they bought less. On the whole, however, that money grew at a very good clip, especially when we were able to add to our car fund every windfall we received. The tax refund went in there, as did some unusual Christmas gifts from our family.

We had planned to keep our car-savings program running for about three years, but the mutual fund we had selected performed so well that after only a year and a half we had a cash value of about $9,500. This was more than enough to buy a used Dodge Caravan. After some diligent searching we found a three-year-old Caravan with about forty-five thousand miles. We could buy it (including tax and licensing—often overlooked in pricing) for about $8,000— much less than we had saved.

Consider what our situation would have been had we taken out a loan to buy the car—assuming we could even get a loan for a used car with so many miles. (Until very recently auto lenders were not inclined to lend on anything older than two years with more than thirty thousand miles or so.) Let's assume that we had borrowed $8,000 at 13 percent, to be paid off over four years. That would require a monthly payment of $215 for four years—a total of $10,320. Recall that we paid $300 per month into our car fund for only eighteen months, so our Caravan cost us only $6,400 (including about $1,000 in tax refunds, gifts, etc.). Here's the bottom line: We could have paid nearly twice as much for the same car if we had borrowed instead of saved.

If you want a new car (or at least one that is "new" to you), then begin by paying for it *before* you buy it. You'll save in every way: You'll avoid interest payments, keep the increase from your investments, and have the bargaining advantage in being able to pay cash for a car.

Perhaps the thought of buying somebody else's problems depresses you, yet you realize that new cars represent a huge financial loss due to depreciation. "I know!" you say, "I'll just lease!" If that is what you are thinking, please go into the bathroom and splash some cold water on your face. Then come back and absorb a dose of painful reality.

Think about the way a lease works. You pay a car dealer enough money for the term of the lease so at the end of that time he can unload the car at a wholesale auction and *still* make a hefty profit. This fact alone should make the buyer wary!

Leasing for the consumer is the worst of all possible worlds. You pay all the depreciation for the term of the lease (and then some), but you don't even get to keep the car when you're done. After paying for the bulk of the car's value, you have to give it back to the dealer. For the dealer, it's great—he gets a ton of money at no risk (because you pay for comprehensive insurance coverage), and he gets the car back to boot. He can wholesale it and recover another big chunk of money to beef up his end of the bottom line. And if you violate the terms of the lease (driving more than twelve thousand miles per year, failing to perform scheduled service, etc.), there are hefty penalties, which all translate into dealer profits. The bottom line on leasing is simple: The dealer makes money—lots of it—and the buyer pays it all.

But if leasing is such a lousy deal, then why is it so popular with consumers? you may wonder. Here's the great attraction as I see it: The buyer gets a new car for what seems like an affordable monthly payment. Presto—instant gratification! And the buyer is insulated from the realities of this lousy financial deal by the passage of time. Only at the end of the lease term will he have to deal with the penalties for driving more miles than the lease allows, and that cost can often be bundled into the next lease contract. The painful fact of having no car at the end of the contract is sugarcoated by the opportunity of leasing yet another new car! Besides, many buyers console themselves with the thought that their lease includes an option to buy—an option that almost always turns out to be a sucker deal compared to buying a similar car on the open market.

Aren't there any situations when leasing a car might be a good idea? If a person is determined to have a new car at all times, regardless of the financial side of the equation, then it might make sense to lease. Or if one's money is tied up in long-term (and very profitable) investments, it might make sense to lease rather than siphon off that money to buy a car.

Think of leasing this way: It is almost the financial equivalent of buying a new car and trading it in every two years (at a significant loss, by the way!). How is this true? Regardless of financial details, buying a new car every few years means that most of your car payments goes into depreciation, not transportation. A Christian who is committed to wisely managing God's assets would not frequently encounter a situation in which a lease represents good stewardship.

Believe it or not, it is possible to have transportation without having a car. But unless you live in Manhattan or Amish country, the inconvenience of not having a car makes automobile ownership almost a necessity. Poor choices in car ownership, however, will have a ripple effect into other financial areas. A single, really unwise decision (say, for example, a lease on a new luxury sport utility vehicle) can have a huge impact on your future finances, even to the point of making it impossible to buy a home or to put your children through college.

So think through your expectations and needs when it comes to car ownership. Do you really need new—or would used do just fine? Are you willing to make the sacrifices necessary to pay cash for your vehicle? What's your personal commitment to keeping your car in good working order once you have it? Can you find creative ways to provide alternate means of transportation that would not require a second car? It may be that the ideal car for you is a bicycle! And a final word of advice: Stay away from those new car lots!

Chapter 27

The Joys of Thriftiness

I'll be the first to admit that I'm not a naturally thrifty person. I mentioned previously that Kathy and I are more like the ant and the grasshopper in Aesop's fable. It was this difference in spending attitudes that drove us to implement an envelope budgeting system, and in particular to make one of the categories "Ray's Allowance." That single decision probably did more to help me develop thriftiness than anything else. When I knew that I had only a few dollars every pay period to spend on whatever wasn't covered by a basic budget category, then I knew I had better make those bucks go a long, long way!

There are a great many things we can all do to bring thrift into our lifestyles. As I've pointed out in these pages, most of us can often do with less—or at least less expensive—and still live joyfully. But some people take living on "less" to an extreme that I don't think is necessarily what God has in mind.

There is a big difference between thrift and miserliness. Guess which attitude a distant relative of mine displayed when he chose to actually drill and fill his own cavities to avoid the expense of having to pay a dentist! Or consider the gentleman with whom I once spent two weeks sharing a flat in the former Soviet Union who carried the idea of thrift a bit too far. In our common bathroom where we hung our towels and washcloths I found a strand of dental floss. I flicked it into the toilet, touching it only with the stick end of my toothbrush. Finished in the bathroom, I abdicated it to my roommate, who shortly howled, "Where's my floss?!" It seems he was in the practice of using only a single strand each week!

Being thrifty is not being miserly, cheap, or fearful of never having enough; rather, it is making the wisest use of God's resources. Our culture doesn't place much value on the virtue of thrift. The very word conjures up images of maiden aunts darning socks or Ebenezer Scrooge refusing to build a fire so young Bob Cratchit could warm his freezing feet. But in the theology of stewardship I've been presenting throughout this book, the only important possession is ourselves, and it is God who is the owner. We don't own anything, but we do have the privilege of choosing how to spend that which God entrusts to us. Thrift should be a guiding principle in making those choices.

Perhaps the best place to start being more thrifty is by considering ways to "buy used." Many people, however, have a prejudice against buying used things. I remember as a child overhearing a neighbor speak contemptuously of a coworker: "He bought that Ford used!" Another acquaintance had been raised on the mission field and spoke with loathing of the "missionary barrels" from which she and her family were dressed and equipped. She had vowed that she would never buy anything that wasn't new—ever! I believe that her unfortunate childhood experience led her to pass up some great values later in life.

When Kathy and I were newlyweds, we were desperately short of basic furniture. Instead of buying new—and it was all too easy, with many stores offering to furnish our house on easy credit terms— we bought used. Our bedroom set was purchased for almost nothing, but we didn't care for its unfashionable pale-blond finish. We later refinished it a somewhat garish royal blue with gold highlights, but it suited us at the time. We also greatly delighted in hiding hearts and "KB xxx RA" and other messages in hidden nooks and crannies of the furniture!

Did you know there are clothing boutiques where fine brand-names can be bought for a fraction of their original cost? Doesn't it make sense to buy more quality for less money, regardless of whether or not the item is used? Garage sales, flea markets, and thriftshops can be especially important sources for equipping a new family. We had fun furnishing our first few homes with treasures we found at garage sales. We bought much of our children's first clothes at thriftshops. Many of my high-tech hobby projects were constructed using bits and pieces found at flea markets. And don't overlook local buy-sell newspapers. These are often chock full of great stuff at low prices—and it never hurts to negotiate with the seller for an even lower price either.

There are often low-cost (or free) alternatives to spending as well. Consider using the public library to borrow videos and CDs (not to mention books!) rather than buying or renting them, and become acquainted with your local theater and musical groups. Many communities and schools sponsor free concerts, recitals, dramatic productions, art exhibits, lectures, and the like that are far richer in texture than the typical movie experience.

One thing modern families often neglect when it comes to living thriftily is the spending category we all need to fund: food. A good portion of the money we've earmarked for daily living expenses can literally be eaten up by our spending habits related to food.

For example, I love eating out. But frequent restaurant dining is the all-time champ of budget-busters. In our first years of marriage I would constantly propose that we abandon whatever was on the stove and try a new restaurant. "Hon, have you ever had Czech food?" I would enthuse, not noticing the steely glint lurking in Kathy's eyes or the dinner she'd already half-prepared on the kitchen stove. When we began to implement the envelope budget, it freed both of us to enjoy eating out, because—for once—we had specifically set aside money for that purpose.

Kathy and I also learned quickly that the only way to stay within our budget assigned to the "groceries" envelope was to keep me away from the supermarket. When Kathy shopped, she did so from a specific list of true needs. If it wasn't on the list, it just wasn't bought. And if there was a cheaper brand than the major name-brand, she bought it. On the occasions when I did the grocery shopping, however, I would invariably come home with a host of interesting prepackaged meals, jars of intriguing sauces, high-calorie cereals, name-brand marmalade, odd fruit or vegetables imported from who knows where, and many other foolish purchases. I'll admit, I had to do some adjusting. My bachelor days had not trained me for eating thriftily. I had received no training in cooking, and sometimes I complained when Kathy substituted a cheaper off-brand for a favorite name-brand. Still, we learned to stay within our budget, and by eating cheaply at home we could thoroughly enjoy eating out occasionally.

Developing an attitude of thrift is essential for living joyfully within your income. It should not, however, be based on selfish tight-fistedness, but on the wide-eyed expectancy that God will meet all of your needs. It's easy to walk into any major store and buy almost anything on credit, but where in that is the hand of God's provision?

One of the joys of being parents is that of giving gifts to our beloved children. When Kathy and I were raising our kids, it was our great delight to seek out their hearts' desires and surprise them with the gifts they really wanted. I don't think our heavenly Father is any less delighted to give good gifts to his children, but we seldom give him the opportunity.

One of the earliest lessons Kathy and I learned in this regard was when we found that our newly assigned air force housing did not include a working washing machine. At first we considered buying a new washer on credit but then had a better idea. We began to pray that God would meet our needs and also began to search in all the likely places for a good used washer. One evening we were playing bridge at the local recreation center and somehow our need came up. One of the ladies at the bridge table had a nonworking washing machine that she would let us have for nothing—all we needed to do was fix it.

I wasn't looking for a fixer-upper, but the fact that we had been praying for a washing machine, and here was one presented on a silver platter, convinced us to accept her offer. With the help of a friend and his pickup truck, we got the washer home and unloaded it in our garage. To my surprise it was designed not only to wash clothes, but also to dry them! As it turned out, a $10 belt from Sears fixed it up, and we happily used it for the balance of our air force career.

Combining an attitude of expectancy with a thrifty lifestyle is a lot more fun and exciting than just plunking down money whenever you need something. Living thriftily introduces an element of delightful expectation into everyday life. It gives God the freedom to surprise us with the overwhelming riches of his provision. We don't want to be like small children who ruin their appetites on cheap candy only moments before their surprise birthday party. By cultivating an attitude of thrift we can let God give us his best.

Chapter 28

Taking the High Road

As a sophomore at Duke University, shortly after I trusted Christ as my Savior, I heard several students speak of how God had blessed them since they'd become Christians. Their grades improved. They found parking places just when they needed them. And they seemed to have just enough money to cover all their expenses. I found myself interested in what I perceived as these tangible "benefits" of becoming a Christian, but I had no desire to see my moral or ethical standards improved! That is exactly what happened, though—and I found out to my shock that my values drastically changed as I grew in Christ.

When I was a senior at Duke, I had an advanced physics laboratory report that wasn't coming out right, and so I "adjusted" the numbers to fit what the theory required. My grade was a solid "B," and I wanted it to stay that way. If I confessed my cheating, however, the consequences could be enormous: failing the course, being suspended by the judicial board, losing my ROTC deferment, and getting drafted into the military. I reasoned that I would certainly wind up dead in a Vietnamese rice paddy if I tried to undo my cheating.

I spent two miserable days struggling against doing what I knew was the right thing to do. Finally, despite my misgivings, I went to the professor and made a clean breast of things. He was astounded by my story, but instead of denouncing me to the judicial board, he just instructed me, "Don't do it again!" I didn't fail the course, lose my scholarship, or get sent to Vietnam—but the turmoil of those days taught me a valuable lesson. Now that I was a child of God, my moral standards were not only my business but his!

Have you ever found a quarter in a pay phone or soda machine? What did you do with it? I've always said, "Thank you!" and put it happily in my pocket or added another quarter to it and bought a Coke. Once, though, Kathy found a woman's wristwatch that appeared more than ordinarily valuable when we were camping in Yellowstone Park. Although we had no way of discovering its owner, we believed that the only right thing to do was to leave it with the authorities in case the owner turned up. As it turned out, that's exactly what happened.

Most people, I believe, would have done the same thing—but why? What makes people decide whether or not to behave with integrity? I believe that Christians, especially, should understand clearly why honesty and integrity are called for in all their dealings. Integrity should characterize every exchange we have with others—in gifts, purchases, and every kind of financial transaction.

Integrity is related to the word "wholeness," and a Christian is whole, or complete, in Christ. This is the theological basis for behaving with integrity: We need nothing because we have everything in Christ. It's not necessary to cut any ethical corners in our financial dealings because to be a Christian means to be "in Christ" and to have his righteousness as our own. Because his Spirit lives within us, we are empowered to imitate him in our daily lives.

Integrity characterized Jesus' life. Just as Superman could convert a chunk of coal into a diamond whenever he needed some cold cash, Jesus could have—without any ethical qualms—drawn whatever wealth he desired from the natural realm. Why didn't he? Evidently, being both God and man involved the requirement to perform miracles only on his Father's timetable and using only his Father's power, not his own.

Try to imagine, if you can, that Jesus is on his way home from his dad's carpentry shop. He stops by the first-century equivalent of the 7-Eleven to buy some milk and stealthily shoplifts a Butterfinger. That's a pretty absurd picture, isn't it? As his followers, it's equally absurd for us to do anything dishonest, unethical, or illegal. Furthermore, if all of the world's wealth belongs to God and has been entrusted to Jesus, then it is available to us. We don't need to use ungodly methods to access God's wealth, because he freely gives his riches to us, his children.

Consider again the parable of the unjust steward (Luke 16:1-8) who had embezzled his master's resources and was going to lose his job as a result. He believed that his only safety lay in performing yet another shady deal. Accordingly, he gave away much of his master's uncollected debts in order to assure his own financial future. Jesus commended this crook, not because he took the high road of integrity (he plainly didn't), but because he had enough sense to recognize a crisis when he saw one. However, he had reasoned incorrectly. Realizing he was in trouble, he had said, in effect, "I either steal some more or I'm lost." He saw only two choices—one resulting in his destruction, the other leading to an immoral act. For the Christian there is always a superior choice: Trust God.

Many Christians find themselves behaving dishonestly because they fail to seriously investigate this possibility—trusting God when they find themselves between the proverbial rock and a hard place. When they get in a financial jam, they assume that there are only a few choices, all with negative consequences. Thus they often choose the option that seems least overtly destructive, even if it costs them their integrity.

Consider Jean Valjean, the hero of Victor Hugo's *Les Misérables*. His family was facing starvation, and he chose to steal bread rather than let them go hungry. Most people today would agree with his decision, even pronouncing it the only moral solution, but it ignored the third option: trust God to supply his need.

The Lord's Prayer contains the phrase "Give us this day our daily bread" for good reason. We need the basics of life (food, clothing, shelter), and the Lord knows this and has arranged to meet these needs. The author of Psalm 37:25 expressed it this way: "I was young and now I am old, yet I have never seen the righteous forsaken or their children begging bread."

Does this mean that God has never let believers live in poverty or that he insulates them and their children from all harm? Of course not. God sometimes has special purposes for his children that include suffering. Peter goes so far as to say that we should "rejoice that you participate in the sufferings of Christ" (1 Peter 4:13). The point is that as a general principle, God honors us for choosing the path of integrity.

It's ironic that so many Christians take the low road, rather than the way of integrity, for a far less significant reason than feeding their starving children. At least Jean Valjean had a better reason for an immoral act than most of us do!

What are some of the most common situations in which we sometimes fail to behave with integrity? Certainly preparing our income taxes provides an enormous temptation to be less than forthcoming. By fudging only a few figures you can save a great deal of money, and the chances of being caught are actually quite low. Cheating on one's taxes is probably one of the most widespread financial crimes in America today.

Living overseas permanently changed my attitude toward paying taxes, by the way. While living in the Philippines under the dictatorship of Ferdinand Marcos, we discovered that we had to pay local income taxes. We realized that the tax forms relied entirely on our own honesty. There was no method by which the Philippine government could have checked the basis of the figures we reported. In other words, we could have easily cheated, and we would almost certainly not have been caught.

But getting caught was not the reason that we didn't cheat. We had made a commitment to live with integrity in the financial arena, and that meant being scrupulous in paying our taxes. On the other hand, it would have been easy to rationalize a decision to cheat. After all, the tax system under the Marcos regime was corrupt, and it was very likely that a large chunk of the money collected in taxes soon found its way to the pockets (or Swiss bank accounts) of the president and his cronies.

Isn't this very much like the situation Jesus faced when his enemies arranged to ask him a trick question in public? "Is it right to pay taxes to Caesar or not?" (Matthew 22:17). The administration of the Roman government in Palestine was rotten to the core, yet Jesus advocated taking the high road when he said, "Give to Caesar what is Caesar's, and to God what is God's."

Since everything we own is, in fact, God's, we can feel much better about paying our taxes—after all, it's not our money! Our job is to be faithful stewards. Sometimes that means giving to governments or projects that we don't support, but our Christian duty as taxpayers is clear.

There are so many other opportunities to take the low road. They range from the somewhat questionable to the outright larcenous, but they all seem seductively reasonable at the time. Here are a few actual examples of Christians who compromised their integrity for financial gain. The names have been changed to protect the guilty.

- A student was not eligible for college financial aid since her mother and divorced father earned more than the guidelines allowed. By stating that she was living independently of her mother (even though she wasn't), however, she qualified for significant financial aid every year. She didn't see anything wrong with this.

- An administrator was employed by a nonprofit organization whose conditions of employment restricted taking additional part-time employment. Harvey joined a multi-level sales organization despite his employer's policy. He saw no ethical problems with this.

- A mechanic had bought a used car that turned out to have been stripped of its antismog devices. Rather than spend the money to have them restored, he paid a fellow mechanic a few extra bucks to turn a blind eye to the missing parts and issue a smog certificate despite the defective exhaust system.

- A student was frustrated by his computer's aging word-processing software. A friend offered to install a copy of the latest office suite of programs onto Chuck's computer. Neither saw this as a problem because the friend paid for the program, and Chuck was too poor to buy his own copy.

Each of these individuals doubtless believed that he or she had good reasons for failing to take the high road. After all, these aren't serious offenses, are they? But would Jesus agree? In ethically questionable situations, I try to remember to ask myself, "What would Jesus do?" Since I'm by nature pretty much of a scoundrel, I find I need to make a daily commitment to take the moral high road. One thing that helps me make the right choice is to remember that one day all of my days will be over and I'll be standing face to face with my Master. How would I dare explain that I was saving "his" money by cheating on my taxes or stealing software?

As children of the King, we are called to take the high road—the way of integrity—in every one of our financial transactions. Since God owns us, we can be content with what he provides. We don't need to cut ethical corners to save his money. I'm sure that God is more than able to make up anything we may lose by being as honest as he wants us to be.

So freely pay those taxes. If you need something, pay for it, and pay what it's worth. The high road will one day take us into God's presence, so we might as well get used to walking on it!

This is the essence of "living large," isn't it? It's walking joyfully through life in God's presence on our way to a more real fellowship with God than we can even imagine. Along the way, God gives us our daily bread and often quite a lot more. We can freely give away what God has given us and yet prudently reserve some for those days when he will want us to rely on what he has previously given. By living within our means, God blesses us beyond our expectations. By giving generously, we can see God multiply those blessings to others beyond all limitations. By saving prudently, we receive God's hand of protection against an uncertain earthly future while on our way to our heavenly home.

In that home we will experience the fruit of our training in this life, training that comes through learning to handle God's resources both wisely and well. Life's journey is not usually short, so don't be discouraged if training in the disciplines of "living large" takes time. God has given you time and, I hope, encouragement from this little book to make the most of it as you learn to walk contented through this life—giving, saving, and living joyfully on the rest.

About the Author

J. Raymond Albrektson has been on the staff of Campus Crusade for Christ for almost twenty-five years, following four years in the U.S. Air Force. Ray and his wife, Kathy, began their Campus Crusade for Christ service at the University of South Florida and at Ball State University in Muncie, Indiana, where Ray directed the Campus Crusade ministry. Since 1986 Ray has served as associate professor in New Testament at the International School of Theology. Based at the U.S. branch near Rancho Cucamonga, California, International has branches in Africa and Asia as well as extension programs that have taken Ray on teaching trips to more than twenty countries.

Ray earned his bachelor's degree in physics at Duke University in 1970. While earning a master of divinity degree at International, his interest in finances led him to focus his dissertation on the relationship between giving attitudes of Christian workers and their sense of financial adequacy. He went on to earn a doctor of theology degree in New Testament studies at the Asian Baptist Graduate Theological Seminary in the Philippines while helping to plant a branch of International in that country. He has been most recently involved in teaching opportunities in the countries of the former Soviet Union.

The Albrektsons now live in Redlands, California. Their daughter, Laurie, is on the Campus Crusade staff at UCLA, where their son, Josh, is a premed student.

For more of Ray's insights on living large, you can send e-mail to LivingLarge@albrektson.com or visit his Web site at http://www.albrektson.com/LivingLarge.